THE CAUSE IS MANKIND

A Liberal Program for
Modern America

HUBERT H. HUMPHREY

A MANOR BOOK, 1978

Manor Books, Inc.
432 Park Avenue South
New York, New York 10016

Library of Congress Catalog Card Number: 64-24012

ISBN CODE 0-532-15324-X

CONTENTS

Acknowledgments

This book represents a personal expression of my views on subjects of paramount importance to me. Yet no man can claim to understand the issues of our times without acknowledging an immense debt to his wife, parents, teachers, students, friends, and associates who have sought to guide and enrich his understanding. My own obligations and indebtedness for such insights as I have are immeasurable.

Some of the material used in this book is based on private or public statements I have made in recent years; and I would like to acknowledge the fine editorial assistance of Morton Puner, whose exhaustive study and editing of my public papers have helped bring this book to life.

Frederick A. Praeger, publisher of *The Cause Is Mankind*, uses these words of Spinoza as his firm's credo: "I have made a ceaseless effort not to ridicule, not to bewail, nor to scorn human actions, but to understand them." I can think of no more eloquent expression of my own aim.

Foreword

John F. Kennedy often quoted Tom Paine's words of 1776 — "the cause of America is in a great measure the cause of all mankind." But in the revolution of the 1960's, he added, the cause of all mankind is the cause of America and "what we do here affects what people will do every place."

This book is about what we do here. It addresses itself to the theme of victory over the challenges that face us. But it is not meant to be a statement of warlike defiance or a call to arms. It does not call for the conquest of one group or one world by another. Instead, it focuses on the struggle President Kennedy talked about and President Johnson continues: the struggle for the triumph of the American spirit, humane and democratic, and the triumph of mankind over its traditional enemies — poverty, hunger, disease, and ignorance. For I believe that with an informed, common-sense, and compassionate approach — the liberal approach, if you will — the American future will be wonderful to behold. And despite the red glare of a sky filled with modern rockets, the members of the family called man will prevail and live in freedom — all three billion of us.

A NATION EULOGIZES HUBERT HORATIO HUMPHREY (1911 - 1978)

"From time to time, our nation is blessed by the presence of men and women who bear a mark of greatness, who help us see a better vision of what we can become. Hubert Humphrey was such a man."

President Carter, from the Presidential retreat at Camp David, Maryland, upon learning of Senator Humphrey's death.

"All my public career I've been closer to this man. Perhaps above all, he showed us all how to die with dignity, with courage, with spirit and with meaning."

Vice President Walter Mondale, in his first public comments after learning of the death of the man he regarded as a "second father."

"Hubert was an idealist in the purest sense. He was a man of character, compassion, enthusiasm, dedication and tremendous ability."

Former President Gerald R. Ford

"Hubert Humphrey commanded the genuine respect and affection of his political opponents and allies alike."

Former President Richard M. Nixon, who returned to Washington for the first time since his resignation to honor his former rival. Mr. Humphrey had phoned Mr. Nixon during the last week of the Senator's life to wish him a happy birthday.

"In New York, former Vice President Nelson A. Rockefeller said Mr. Humphrey would be remembered for achieving progress in human rights while 'winning the love and respect of the American people.' He added that the Senator was a 'great human being' who had 'great spirit and consummate courage.' "

New York Times, January 15, 1978

"He was a great American who belonged to the world because the values he upheld were universal. The British people extend their deepest sympathy."

Prime Minister James Callaghan
of Great Britain

"The late Senator Humphrey was a man of dedication to the cause of world peace and the welfare of men . . . His death was not only a profound loss for your compatriots, but also a source of deep sorrow for millions of people of the world."

Prime Minister Takeo Fukuda of Japan

THE HAPPY LEGACY OF HUBERT H. HUMPHREY

"Hubert H. Humphrey and death seemed intrinsically incompatible. Few human beings have ever been in love with life or enjoyed life's challenge and variety more than he did. He gave unstintingly of his heart, mind, imagination and physical energy, and he left America a better country for his efforts . . .

"In his ill-fated Presidential campaign in 1968, Humphrey was derided for his slogan "The Politics of Happiness." But to those who knew him, the term was an accurate and sincere reflection of his personality. He was truly a cheerful, bouncy, warmhearted man who wished good things for all God's children."

New York Times

"He had a profound and lasting effect...Throughout his career he was able to perceive rich possibilities where others observed but obstacles."

Senator Robert C. Byrd, Democrat of
West Virginia and Senate Majority Leader

"He was a man of the people and one of the greatest senators of all time. He was far ahead of the country on domestic issues."

Thomas P. O'Neill, Jr., Speaker of
the United States House of Representatives

"Humphrey was the latest in a distinguished line of Senators, from Henry Clay and Daniel Webster to Robert La Follette and Arthur Vandenberg, whose impact on public life was greater than that of most Presidents . . . 'The good old days were never that good, believe me,' he once said. 'The good new days are today, and better days are coming tomorrow. Our greatest songs are still unsung.' Yet many of them were sung by Hubert Horatio Humphrey."

Edwin Warner, *Time* Magazine

"Thirty years ago, he called on his fellow citizens to walk out into the sunlight of human rights . . . He was the most creative lawmaker of his generation."

Senator George McGovern, Democrat of
South Dakota

"The Senate has lost an incomparable leader. The nation and the people have lost a rare spirit, and I have lost a dear friend."

Senator Clifford P. Case, Republican
of New Jersey

"Hubert is probably thinking of the speech he might give if the Almighty permitted him to come back for a few minutes. And he wouldn't be taking this somberly. That voice of his was made for good cheer. It couldn't fit a sad speech."

Senator Edmund S. Muskie, Democrat, Maine, speaking to reporters outside the Capitol rotunda as Senator Humphrey's body lay in state in the Capitol.

"He was always a happy warrior, an unabashed liberal who loved the politics of small towns and the power of Big Government . . . he embraced his friends, he forgave his enemies and he forgot the time whenever he got to talking . . . He bounced back from political defeat with irrepressible energy, and self-deprecating humor, and waged a courageous personal fight against cancer . . . When Hubert Horatio Humphrey Jr. succumbed last week at the age of 66, it was a little hard to believe that his hear-me-my-friends voice and his by-gosh-and-by-golly spirit were finally gone.

"He left behind a legacy of immense goodwill and landmark legislation."

Newsweek report on the death of Mr. Humphrey

The following are the eulogies delivered by President Carter and Vice President Mondale at the memorial service for Senator Humphrey in the United States Capitol.

President Carter

At critical times in our history, the United States has been blessed by great people who just by being themselves give us a vision of what we are at our best and of what we might become. Hubert Humphrey was such a man.

In a time of impending social crisis 30 years ago, his was the first voice I ever heard, a lone voice persistently demanding basic human rights for all Americans.

It was the most difficult moral and social issue that my own generation would have to face. In those early days, his was a clear voice, a strong voice, a passionate voice, which recruited others to join in a battle in our own country so that equal rights of black people could be gained – to vote, to hold a job, to go to school, to own a home.

I first met Humbert Humphrey when he was Vice President, torn because his heart was filled with love and a yearning for peace while at the same time he was meticulously loyal to a President who led our nation during an unpopular war.

I also remember him in a time of political defeat, courageously leading a divided Democratic Party, losing his uphill campaign for President by just a few votes. But he was a big man. And without bitterness, he gave his support to the new President, and then came back later to the Senate to serve his nation once again.

For the last year of his life I knew him best. And that's when I needed him most, despite campaign disagreements and my own harsh words, spoken under pressure and in haste. It was not his nature to forget how to love or to forgive.

He has given me, freely, what I need: the support and understanding of a close and true friend, the advice of a wise and honest counselor.

When he first visited me in the Oval Office, I felt that he should have served there.

I know that he's been an inspiration and a conscience to us all, but especially to the leaders of our nation: to Harry Truman, to Dwight Eisenhower, to John Kennedy, to Lyndon Johnson, to Richard Nixon, to Gerald Ford, and to me.

We and our families are here today to testify that Hubert Humphrey may well have blessed our country more than any of us.

His greatest personal attribute was that he really knew how to love. There was nothing abstract or remote about it. He did not love humanity only in the mass. You could feel it, in the scope of his concerns, in his words, in the clasp of his hands, in the genuine eager interest in his eyes as he looked at you.

He always spoke up for the weak and the hungry and for the victims of discrimination and poverty. He never lost sight of our own human possibilities. He never let us forget that in our democratic nation we are a family, bound together by a kinship of purpose and by mutual concern and respect.

He reminded us that we must always protect and nurture the other members of our national family.

Yesterday as messages poured in to me as President, and to the members of the Humphrey family, from throughout the world, I realized vividly that Hubert Humphrey was the most beloved of all Americans. And that his family had encompassed not just the people of the United States but of all people everywhere.

He asked, as the Vice President has said, that this service

be a celebration. And in a way, that's what it is. Even as we mourn his death, we celebrate because such a man as Hubert Humphrey was among us. The joy of his memory will last far longer than the pain and sorrow of his leaving.

Vice President Mondale

Dear Muriel, the Humphrey family, and guests. There is a natural impulse at a time like this to dwell on the many accomplishments of Hubert Humphrey's remarkable life, by listing a catalogue of past events as though there were some way to quantify what he was all about. But I don't want to do that because Hubert didn't want it and neither does Muriel.

Even though this is one of the saddest moments of my life and I feel as great a loss as I've ever known, we must remind ourselves of Hubert's last great wish, that this be a time to celebrate life and the future, not to mourn the past, and his death.

But, Muriel, I hope you will forgive me if I don't entirely succeed in looking forward and not backward, because I must, for a moment. Two days ago, as I flew back from the West over the land that Hubert loved, and to this city that he loved, I thought back over his life and its meaning. And I tried to understand what it was about this unique person that made him such an uplifting symbol of hope and joy for all people.

And I thought of the letter that he wrote to Muriel over 40 years ago when he first visited Washington. He said in that letter, "Maybe I seem foolish to have such vain hopes and plans. But, Bucky, I can see how, someday, if you and I just apply ourselves and make up our minds to work for bigger things, how we can someday live here in Washington and probably be in government, politics or service. I intend to set my aim at Congress."

Hubert was wrong only in thinking that his hopes and plans might be in vain. They were not, as we all know. Not only did he succeed with his beloved wife at his side, he succeeded gloriously and beyond even his most optimistic dreams. Hubert will be remembered by all of us who served with him as one of the greatest legislators in our history. He will be remembered as one of the most loved men of his time. And even though he failed to realize his greatest goal, he achieved something much more rare and valuable than the nation's highest office. He became his country's conscience.

Today the love that flows from everywhere, enveloping Hubert, flows also to you, Muriel. And the presence today here, where America bids farewell to her heroes, of President and Mrs. Carter, of former Presidents Ford and Nixon, and your special friend and former First Lady, Mrs. Johnson, attest to the love and respect that the nation holds for both of you.

That letter to Bucky, Muriel, also noted three principles by which Hubert defined his life: work, determination and high goals. They were a part of his life's pattern when I first met him 31 years ago. I was only 17, fresh out of high school, and he was the Mayor of Minneapolis. He had then all the other sparkling qualities he maintained throughout his life: boundless good humor, endless optimism and hope, infinite interests, intense concern for people and their problems, compassion without being patronizing, energy beyond belief, and a spirit so filled with love there was no room at all for hate or bitterness. He was simply incredible.

When he said that life was not meant to be endured but, rather, to be enjoyed, you knew what he meant. You could see it simply by watching him and listening to him. When Hubert looked at the lives of black Americans in the 40's, he saw endurance but not enjoyment, and his heart insisted that it was time for Americans to walk forthrightly into the bright sunshine of human rights.

When Hubert looked at the young, who could not get a good education, he saw endurance and not enjoyment. When Hubert saw old people in ill health he saw endurance and not enjoyment. When Hubert saw middle-class people striving to survive and working people without jobs and decent homes, he saw endurance and not enjoyment.

Hubert was criticized for proclaiming the politics of joy, but he knew that joy was essential to us and is not frivolous. He loved to point out that ours is the only nation in the world to officially declare the pursuit of happiness as a national goal.

But he was also a sentimental man, and that was part of his life, too. He cried in public and without embarrassment. In his last major speech in his beloved Minnesota, he wiped tears from his eyes and said: "A man without tears is a man without a heart." If he cried often, it was not for himself but for others.

Above all, Hubert was a man with a good heart, and on this sad day it would be good for us to recall some of Shakespeare's words: "A good leg will fall, a straight back will stoop, a black beard will turn white, a curl'd pate will grow bald, a fair face will wither, a full eye will wax hollow, but a good heart is the sun and the moon. Or, rather, the sun and not the moon for it shines bright and never changes, but keeps his course truly." Hubert's heart kept its course truly.

He taught us all how to hope and how to love, how to win and how to lose: he taught us how to live and finally, he taught us how to die.

"He said to me, 'Look, we're only doing about half of what we should be doing.' He made you realize that there was no limit to what you could do."

J. B. Cardaro, member of Senator Humphrey's staff

"A noble American has been taken from us. No one had higher aspirations for our people and our time, nor a great sympathy for the longings and misfortunes of his fellow Americans than Hubert Humphrey. He leaves us and our nation better and richer for having abided with us a while."

Senator Jacob Javits, Republican of New York

"I only thank God that before he died, his country came to realize how much Hubert Humphrey meant to us all."

Senator Daniel Patrick Moynihan, Democrat of New York

"Hubert Humphrey never made it to the Presidency, and those of us who look back on our times may be tempted to classify him as a secondary figure. But for those who have lived through the three decades since World War II, there was nothing secondary about him. He and Richard M. Nixon dominated those years, the twin colossi of American politics, sometimes in office and sometimes out, but never absent from the calculations of those who trafficked in power."

R. W. Apple Jr., London Bureau chief, *New York Times*, and long-time friend of Mr. Humphrey

"Senator Hubert H. Humphrey represented what was best in America . . . he was always the champion of the underdog."

Douglas Fraser, President of the
United Automobile Workers

"Senator Humphrey was our friend – a genuine supporter of the labor movement in good times and bad."

George Meany, president of the
American Federation of Labor and
Congress of Industrial Organizations

"Throughout his life, Hubert Humphrey was a 'winter soldier' of the American liberal movement. His dreams of the 1940's became the Federal programs of the 1950's and '60's. Through his long and useful career, he taught the rest of us to face difficulty. At the end, he was still teaching us."

Governor Hugh Carey of New York

"I am deeply moved by the death of Senator Humphrey. He served his nation and his beloved Democratic party with skill, wisdom and dignity. He was a good friend, tireless leader and a great American.

"He was continuously responsive to calls for help from the weak and defenseless. His passing leaves a void in the Congress and in our country. He will be sorely missed."

Mayor Edward Koch of New York City

"He was the most outspoken and courageous leader for civil rights in the Senate . . . We have lost a great friend."

Coretta Scott King, widow of the
Reverend Martin Luther King, Jr.

"He was a good man."

Elderly black man waiting in the cold
outside the Capitol to pay his last

respects to the late Senator Humphrey

"Today is an even more special day. Today Hubert comes home to Minnesota for the last time to rest in the place he loved best, in the place which gave him spiritual and political sustenance.

"He was a special man in a special place, and I know he would want me to say today, 'Thank you, Minnesota.' "

The Reverend Calvin W. Didler, delivering his eulogy
to Mr. Humphrey at funeral services at
the House of Hope Presbyterian Church
in St. Paul, Minnesota, on January 15, 1978.

"If he seems loquacious, be patient with him, Lord, as we have always been, because he most always had a good point."

The Rev. Didler, in his benediction after
the long, two-hour service filled with music –
the "celebration" Mr. Humphrey himself had requested.

"We have lost a voice that warmed, cheered, amused, consoled, inspired and spoke so often with so much compassion for the conscience of a whole nation. We have lost a giant who strode gently across our political landscape, a man whose greatness was rooted perhaps in his obvious human flaws and frailties.

"By golly, Hubert, we're going to miss you, terribly. Bless your heart."

Mel Elfin, Washington Buearu
Chief, *Newsweek*.

I

Freedom: A Personal Appraisal

Professor John P. Roche, a distinguished fellow political scientist and good friend, recently wrote that Americans have made such great changes in their attitudes toward civil rights and civil liberties in the past fifty years that we have just now produced one of the greatest breakthroughs in human freedom. The "good old days," Professor Roche believes, were mainly a myth, and only a relative few enjoyed the freedoms called for by American tradition and philosophy. He goes on to say that it was not the eighteenth or the nineteenth century but the twentieth — really the mid-twentieth — century that gave the United States its authentic birth of freedom for all.

It is true — and good — that today there is a clamor and a demand for justice such as we have never heard before. The demand is urgent and must be heeded. We, the people of the nation with the most advanced technology on earth, are still benighted in many of our attitudes toward race. But this is one of the aberrants of American life, not its mainstream.

The original and basic birth of freedom in America, of course, took place long before this century. I know because I am one of its legatees. The America I was born into in 1911 was vastly different in many ways from the America of today — but not in essence.

In many ways, to me, my father typifies that essential spirit. He read a good deal of Tom Paine, Benjamin Franklin, and Thomas Jefferson. In his mind, the Civil War was fought over the issues of preservation of the Union *and* the freeing of the slaves. In my boyhood hometown of Doland, South Dakota, my father was involved in the great local fight over the issue of selling the municipally owned power and light company to a private firm. He believed that our town should own its utilities, but his side lost. He was a hard-working, enterprising small businessman.

He had an intense interest in civic affairs, and it was probably his influence that led me to become a college teacher of political science and then a practicing politician. He loved America, but saw its imperfections and believed that community action and the government could correct them. He thought that in a country so blessed with natural resources, men should be able to make a decent living from their own labor. He wanted all people to walk proudly, in dignity, as he did. He was incapable of prejudice for reason of color or creed.

My father was hardly a loner or a rebel against his times. He was a product of all that had gone before — a child of the freedom long developing in this nation, of the American humane spirit.

I do believe, however, that freedom has grown enormously in the past half-century. This is an astonishing fact, a tribute to the vitality of our institutions, when you look at the outlines of the history of the era. In those fifty years, we've gone through two World Wars and several minor but deadly ones; a Depression that lasted the better part of a decade; a proliferation of extremist movements of the right and left, here and abroad; the rise of totalitarian systems of unprecedented strength and horror; the Cold War of the nuclear age; such phenomena as the Ku Klux Klan, McCarthyism, and blacklists; the murder of a beloved President.

And yet, democracy has weathered all these threats to freedom. On the balance, today, our civil liberties and civil rights appear to be at least as secure as they ever have been — and, in some conspicuous cases, much more secure.

We plead for progress, for greater understanding, for a more compassionate approach to our own and to world problems. We must always be aware of our defects and not try to hide them. But let us not forget this great reality of national life. We do have more freedom than ever before. Greater freedom in important areas: freedom of choice, freedom to get a better education, freedom to find a better job, freedom of access to more information through better systems of communications, freedom from the psychological entrapments of prejudice and dogma.

Most of us have greater mobility — physical, social, cultural.

We are rich in many such types of freedom. As a nation, we have never lost the dream of opportunity for all.

II

The Quest of Liberalism

The concept of liberalism as we know it in America today has evolved through centuries of history. It is still evolving, as society and its problems and challenges develop and change. One of its basic tenets — that freedom is essential for the full realization of the individual personality — is deeply rooted in religion and philosophy. It was expressed by the Greek philosophers, by the Hebrew prophets, and in the Sermon on the Mount.

The doctrine of the innate natural rights of the individual was expounded by both the Cynics and the Stoics in the ancient world. And during the long night of feudalism, it was expanded and systematized by St. Thomas Aquinas for the medieval church — eventually to become the philosophical basis for the eighteenth-century struggles for political freedom.

In the meantime, however, after the fall of the Roman Empire, society as a whole assumed a static hierarchical pattern. Virtually no one was recognized by the ruling classes as having any rights as an individual human being. Rather, according to his status in the hierarchy, whether serf or lord, a man had rights and obligations which attached to that status. No matter how able he was, he could not rise above his status; no matter how inept, he could not fall below it.

It would be hard to imagine a system better designed to prevent progress — and little progress, in fact, took place. Instead, there was stagnation, punctuated occasionally by desperate and futile uprisings by the serfs. Yet, even in these centuries of darkness, some candles burned. Christ and the Hebrew prophets still spoke from the pages of the Bible, and Greek and Latin manuscripts kept alive, for the small minority who could read them, the wisdom and knowledge of earlier days.

It was the gradual growth of towns, and of a class of merchants and skilled craftsmen within them, that eventually broke the iron grip of feudalism. The townspeople — able to rise and prosper, within limits, according to their abilities — chafed under the myriad of feudal restrictions, which prevented them from rising further.

Moreover, a growing number of them, now literate, took up the cause of freedom, which, like seed in the winter soil, had long lain dormant. The whole fabric of English feudalism was challenged, for example, by a Biblically inspired scrap of doggerel:

> When Adam delved and Eve span
> Who was then the gentleman?

But the high walls of the feudal Jericho did not fall at a single trumpet blast. In fact, the urban middle class had to wage a struggle that took centures — and, indeed, was not everywhere ultimately successful. First, it allied itself with kings to break the power of the feudal nobles and reduce them to mere dependents of the court. Then, often in alliance with the smaller rural landowners, it broke the power of the kings. It was such an alliance between rural gentry like Cromwell and the London merchants that toppled King Charles I from his throne.

I had briefly summarized these developments of hundreds of years in order to place American liberalism in its historical context. The American Revolution of 1776 was, in fact, the first permanently successful revolution against the power of kings. It represented the culmination, among Europeans transplanted to a new world, of centuries of struggle by their ancestors; and it was also the beginning of a new era in history. Philosophers had written that all men were created equal; now, for the first time, a nation was founded foursquare upon this revolutionary concept.

It is therefore understandable that, even among those who approved the incorporation of these words about the equality of men in the Declaration of Independence, some did not realize their full implications. For example, some viewed the Negro slaves as chattels, or at least as an inferior breed of men; even Jefferson himself only came to realize later, through personal experience, that Negroes given the same freedom and advantages as white men could develop the same abilities.

Also, it may be noted that the Founding Fathers said that men were "created" equal; they did not say they would remain equal. Here we see the other side of the coin of early liberalism; if men were free to rise according to their abilities, they were also free to fall. Actually, Jefferson and his followers did not expect them to rise very high or to fall very low; his vision of America was of a country of small and medium farmers, made roughly equal by the fact of their ownership of land.

Also, in its fullest sense, the freedom the middle class had won was freedom for its own members — freedom that is, for the merchants, professional people, and skilled craftsmen in the towns and for landowners in the countryside. Many of the Founding Fathers regarded with horror the idea that unskilled urban workers and farm laborers might have a voice in government; the franchise in the colonies, and later in the states, was granted only to those who had certain minimum income or property-ownership qualifications.

Fortunately, however, in this New World the tide of equalitarianism ran very strong; within a generation, universal male suffrage had become the prevailing principle. This extension of the vote to all free men proved a great and enduring blessing to American democracy.

In contrast, liberalism in Europe sometimes took the form of a singularly dogmatic and pitiless doctrine. Its limitations were starkly revealed by the Industrial Revolution. Intoxicated by the opportunities the machine offered to expand production and create wealth, orthodox European liberals tended to be ruthlessly indifferent to the suffering the machine caused. Despite the shocking conditions in which the works lived and toiled — the dismal slums, the ignorance, the poverty, the disease, the prevalence of child labor — they rejected any intervention of government on behalf of the poor as contrary to the known and immutable laws of economic growth. And the poor, having no vote and no unions, were at first defenseless. Indeed, if they received any sympathy and help, it was more often from the conservative aristocracy, among whom the feudal tradition of *noblesse oblige* — that is, that the higher orders of society had certain minimum obligations to the lower — still persisted.

It was no wonder that freedom so narrowly defined had a bitter taste for the poor. Liberty without equality, Hobhouse thundered, was nothing but "a name of noble sound and squalid results." And as Anatole France put it: "The law, in its majestic equality, forbids the rich as well as the poor to sleep under bridges, to beg in the streets, and to steal bread."

Liberalism in Europe did evolve and did move somewhat with the times; but it moved too little and too late. As the urban workers won the right to vote and organized themselves into unions to defend their interests, they turned to socialism, either in its democratic form or in its totalitarian perversion, Communism. Liberal parties still exist in Europe, but they run a poor third to the conservative right and the socialist or Communist left.

It has been its ability to move with the times that has enabled American liberalism to gain and hold the allegiance of the great majority of the less privileged, and to forestall the rise of significant socialist and Communist parties. American liberalism is in the authentic liberal tradition, in that it sees free competitive enterprise as the mainspring of economic life and is dedicated to the maintenance of the traditional freedoms of speech, of the press, of assembly, and the like. But it has moved beyond the old liberal dogma that *that* government is best which governs least. It sees many positive roles for government to perform — both in setting a general framework of growth in which private enterprise can flourish and in establishing minimum living standards for all people.

American liberalism, unlike European liberalism, proved capable of coping with the problems of the new industrial society that came into being here in the latter part of the nineteenth century. Instead of uncritically welcoming the new concentrations of wealth and power that emerged, it recognized the danger that they would be used to control and cripple government, destroy competition, and increase the maldistribution of wealth. It saw in them the seeds of a new menace to freedom, as threatening to the freedom of the individual as the power of a seventeenth-century king.

The new liberalism therefore began to press government to intervene and restore a balance in society. It understood that the same forces which had released the productive energies of Western society now threatened to restrain them, and that the forces which had once demolished the power of despots now nourished a new despotism.

Universal male suffrage and the equalizing effect of expanding frontiers helped American liberalism to make a historic breakthrough into the twentieth century and to establish itself as a dominant political force. So also did a series of outstanding statesmen who shaped liberalism into an instrument capable of dealing with an industrial society. They included Theodore Roosevelt, who first saw the democratic possibilities in big government and the need to use it to cope with problems raised by big business; Woodrow Wilson, who continued the work that the first Roosevelt had begun; and

Franklin D. Roosevelt, who completed the transformation of American liberalism from its original anti-statism to a doctrine embracing the use of the power of the state to achieve both freedom and a reasonable measure of equality.

President Franklin Roosevelt made this observation about liberalism in 1938:

> In Jefferson's day, in Jackson's day, and in Lincoln's and Theodore
> Roosevelt's and Wilson's day, one group
> emerged clearly as liberals opposed
> to the other — the conservatives. One great difference which has characterized
> this division has been that the liberal party — no matter what its particular
> name was at the time — believed in the wisdom and efficacy of the will of the
> great majority of the people, as distinguished from the judgment of a small minority
> of either education or wealth. The liberal group has alwasy believed that control
> by a few — political or economic control — if exercised for a long period of time,
> would be destructive of a sound representative democracy. For this reason, for
> exacmple, it has always advocated the extension of the right of suffrage to as many
> people as possible . . .
>
> The other great difference between the two parties has been this: The liberal
> party is a party which believes that, as new conditions and problems arise

beyond the power of men and women to meet as individuals, it becomes the duty of the government itself to find new remedies with which to meet them . . . That
theory of the role of government was expressed by Abraham Lincoln when he said that
"the legitimate object of government is to do for a community of people whatever
they need to have done, but cannot do at all, or cannot do so well, for themselves,
in their separate and individual capacities."

Because they concern themselves thoughtfully with unique problems, liberals often disagree. Once, when he was asked why the conservatives always seemed united and the liberals divided, F.D.R. remarked that the answer was simple: "There are many ways of going forward, but only one way of standing still."

Thus, as Americans confronted the new problems of the concentration of private economic powers, two schools of liberal thought and action emerged. The first believed that bigness in itself was evil, and that large concentrations of power should be broken up by government action — i.e., by "trust-busting" — wherever they existed.

The other school, which emerged somewhat later, held that in certain fields bigness and the mobilization of resources it makes possible are essential to progress in an economy that increasingly requires mass production and mass distribution. While recognizing the dangers inherent in such concentrations of wealth, some liberals held that they should be dealt with by countervailing power — the power of the government to regulate and control, on the one hand, and the power of organized labor and other private groupings on the other.

As the memoirs of the New Deal period make clear, both schools of thought were powerfully represented in the early years of the Roosevelt Administration — sometimes one was dominant, sometimes the other. Yet, as liberalism developed into the later phase of the New Deal, through the Truman and Kennedy years and into the Johnson Administration, it became increasingly clear that there were essential truths in both views, and that they were not, in fact, incompatible.

Big business does have an essential contribution to make to our economy; so, too, does small business. Where the concentration of economic power is such that it is not adequately contained by countervailing forces elsewhere in the economy, the government has a clear duty to act. Otherwise, it can best maintain the needed balance in our economy by fostering competition and the growth of small business; by seeing to it that the unions are able to maintain their bargaining power; and by ensuring the survival of the family farm in the face of a trend toward large-scale "factory" farming.

This concept is often called the "mixed economy." I should prefer to call it the "balanced economy." In such an economy, where big business and small, capital and labor, factory farmer and family farmer all have roles to play, there will of course be conflicts and struggles for advantage; without such conflicts and struggles, our economy would lack its native vigor. But, within a context of over-all growth policies set by the government, these are conflicts that can be resolved, to the benefit of all and the actual detriment of none.

An essential counterpart to the balanced economy is a welfare program in which the government takes the responsibility — a responsibility that it alone can adequately fulfill — for seeing to it that a decent standard of living and of human dignity is assured to every American citizen. The foundations of the humanitarian state were laid by the New Deal; President Johnson has moved to complete the task by declaring — and by waging with his characteristic dedication and energy — an all-out war against the poverty that still persists, even in our affluent society.

While the liberal parties remain weak in Europe, liberalism as an approach to the problems of society has made a dramatic comeback there in recent years. Virtually all the Western European socialist parties are by now liberal (in the American sense) in all but name, having shed most of their earlier dogmatic baggage. Even in the Soviet Union, after almost a half-century of Communism, some basic ideas of liberalism are beginning to assert themselves. A growing minority of young Russians are demanding greater freedom of speech and action;

a growing minority of economists and technicians are saying that the Soviet system offers too little scope for individual initiative and enterprise. These are as yet small cracks in the Soviet monolith, but they are the same kind of cracks which, beginning in a small way in the seemingly impregnable edifice of feudalism, eventually brought it crashing down.

The state of liberalism in America is good; its appeal in other parts of the world is growing. But we must not for a moment let this infect us with complacency. The enduring strength of American liberalism is that it recognizes and welcomes change as an essential part of life, and moves to seize rather than evade the challenges and opportunities that change presents. It is, basically, an attitude toward life rather than a dogma — characterized by a warm heart, an open mind, and willing hands. Without a warm heart, it would lack its essential sensitivity and responsiveness to the needs and aspirations of people at home and abroad. Without an open mind, it would lack its essential ability to recognize new problems and think through new solutions. Without the willingness to act, and to act boldly, it would lack its characteristic ability to transmute feelings and thoughts into meaningful deeds. That is why I am proud to be a modern American liberal, ever conscious of the great achievements of our past, ever confident about our future.

III

On Human Rights

The Four Freedoms of Franklin Roosevelt implied a fifth one — freedom with dignity. In the year 1964 that fifth freedom has come closer to reality for our Negro citizens.

The United States Supreme Court, in setting aside recently a contempt conviction of Mary Hamilton, a civil-rights worker, addressed itself to a symbolic indignity that is at the heart of the Negro's mood of anger and unrest today — and is sometimes more wounding than poverty itself.

An Alabama Court had convicted Miss Hamilton of contempt because she refused to answer questions when a courtroom prosecutor addressed her as "Mary." Quietly, but firmly, she reminded him that her name was Miss Hamilton. When he persisted, she refused to answer.

Addressing Negroes by their first names in a courtroom or other official setting has been one of the historic ways of treating them as inferiors, members of a lower caste. Negroes have had to accept this extraordinary act of contempt because they have felt powerless to do anything about it.

This is no longer the case. Miss Hamilton's courtroom rebellion shows the resolve of young Negroes to resist being patronized or pushed around. There is a new militancy among Negroes today. And along with it there is a greater resentment of whites because of the ever-broken hopes and promises of the past. These expressions of resentment are more candid and forthright than ever.

Does the slogan "Freedom now" sound too demanding and rebellious? Think how you would feel if it was your freedom at stake, a freedom that you and your ancestors had been deprived of for generations. It is sufficient to note that the Emancipation Proclamation is now more than a hundred years old — and its promise is just now becoming reality; that the Supreme Court's decision on desegregation of the public schools came ten years ago — and in 1964, fewer than 10 per cent of Negro children in the South attend integrated schools.

The new militancy toughens and mobilizes parts of the Negro community that have never before been involved in civil-rights activities. The old established forms of protest and striving for improvement — leaving matters in the hands of experts and lawyers — no longer satisfy great parts of the Negro community, especially the young people.

I am often asked about my views on the morality and worth of the demonstrations — the sit-ins, marches, fasts, and other types of nonviolent activity — that Negro leadership uses in its campaign for "Freedom now." Some of these have been in violation of local laws. I can hardly be expected to condone law-breaking. But

I believe the reasons for the demonstrations must always be examined; they are the core of the problem, not the demonstrations themselves. Until the Supreme Court decided otherwise, Miss Hamilton was technically in violation of a state law. But that was not the point. When Negroes have equal rights and full protection of the law — and that fifth freedom — then the demonstrations, technically legal or not, will cease.

One of the tragedies of today's situation is that the motives of the white liberal community, even the meaning of the Judaeo-Christian tradition, are being seriously questioned by some Negroes. The Black Muslims are perhaps the most dramatic example of various extremist Negro movements that have arisen in reaction to the cruel past. Their appeal is tragically racist; they deny that all men are brothers. If white Northerners feel at all smug about their treatment of Negroes, let them be reminded: The Black Muslim movement is essentially a phenomenon of the urban North, of the Negro ghettos, of poverty, of inadequate education, and — again — of broken promises.

We have made great strides since the end of World War II. But there remains pain and anguish and the continued crippling of the Negro psyche every day. Have we done enough? Is it any wonder that even the word "liberal" is a term of derision for some Negroes today; that they are suspicious that those whites who join in freedom protests and sit-ins are on a lark of sorts or seeking some psychological catharsis?

This failure to win the full confidence of the Negroes presents a real challenge to liberals. The basic challenge, though, is the fight for he achievement of freedom for all. The preamble to the Constitution speaks in the name of "We, the people" — not white people or black people. And that is the way it must be. I had the honor of serving as the Democratic floor manager of the 1964 civil-rights bill, which the Senate debated for many long weeks this spring, finally approving the bill by a large majority and sending it on to President Johnson in mid-summer to be signed into law. This was probably the most significant bill to come before Congress in our lifetime. It is good legislation, much of it addressed to the heart of the problem of discrimination.

But the law can be no better than the people who administer it and the people who are called upon to obey it. In short, its success depends upon the attitudes of all Americans — on their attitudes toward freedom, on the stand they take against prejudice and discrimination.

My speeches have often dealt with the high cost of discrimination. The facts are dismaying. We know that prejudice and racial discrimination have damaged our reputation around the world and have served as a primary excuse for expression of anti-Americanism. But how costly racial prejudice has also been to the American economy at home. These are some of the statistics of the situation:

Income: The average white man's income in

1962 was $5,462. The average Negro's income was $3,023 — 45 per cent less.

Housing: Despite the improvements of the postwar years, the 1960 census showed that only two of five Negro families lived in sound structures with hot and cold running water, a bath or shower, and flush toilet.

Employment: The 1960 census showed that about 3.6 million Negro men were employed. One million worked as laborers; another half-million as janitors, porters, cooks, elevator operators, and the like. These two low-paying occupational groups accounted for about 40 per cent of all the jobs held by Negro men. About 10 percent of Negro men worked as craftsmen. Their average earnings were $3,500, compared with $5,400 for whites. Clerical work, a major source of white-collar employment for Negro men, offers a somewhat better ratio of pay. One reason is that a large proportion of Negro clerical workers are hired by the U.S. Post Office, which does not discriminate. The average Negro clerical worker earns $4.072, while the white gets $4,848. For mail carriers, the average is $5,101 for Negroes and $5,309 for whites.

Education: This has been the traditional route of escape for children of the slums. Although education has not helped Negroes as much. In New York City, 69 per cent of the Negroes do not have a high-school diploma; the figure is only slightly lower for whites — 62 per cent are not high-school graduates. But whites are twice as successful in earning a living. Only last year, the Senate Committee on Labor and Public Welfare determined that the Negro who has finished four years of college can expect a lifetime income of $185,000. Yet a white man with only an eighth-grade education can expect a lifetime income of $191,000. Negroes are fully aware of these discrepancies. It is not surprising that education, as an escape from poverty, does not seem to offer the same inducement to many Negroes that it has in the past offered to less visible and put-upon minorities.

If we could fully train and educate the Negro population in the United States — and if we could eliminate the racial barriers in employment, housing, and elsewhere — this would be a much wealthier nation in terms of money alone. The President's Council of Economic Advisers has reported that racial bias costs the country $13-17 billion a year in increases in our gross national product. This is more than a fourth of the amount we spend for national defense. It is three times as much as we spend on our space program. And this loss in income does not, of course, take into account what we pay in a higher crime rate, poor health, urban decay, mounting welfare needs, and countless other costs arising out of discrimination.

To the vast majority of Negroes, the issue of civil rights is directly tied to the problems of jobs and education. The most immediate problem for all too many Negroes is finding a job that pays enough to feed, clothe, and house their families. It is vital to have good civil-rights laws concerning public accommodations and the like on the books. But to paraphrase one of comedian Dick Gregory's best lines, it doesn't mean a heck of a lot that you can sit at a lunch counter if you don't have a dime for a cup of coffee.

The issue of civil rights is far more than a legal or an economic issue, however. It is a moral issue, transcending considerations of political party and self-interest. It is tragic that few men in positions of leadership, before the administration of John F. Kennedy, put it in those terms. President Kennedy did; so, too, did President Lyndon B. Johnson in his State of the Union Message.

President Johnson's firm leadership on civil rights appears to have surprised those who had forgotten his record. They failed to remember that his idol and mentor was Franklin Roosevelt. They failed to remember that he became thoroughly familiar with, and was revolted by, the ugly patterns of discrimination against Mexican-Americans when he was a young schoolteacher in south Texas. They failed to remember that he was *not* among the signers of the Southern Manifesto in 1956. And they did not give him enough credit for initiating and engineering the passage of the civil-rights bills of 1957 and 1960 — the only two civil-rights bills, aside from the latest one, that we've had in the past hundred years.

This is hardly an easy political feat for a man from a state that was once part of the Confederacy. But just as we tend to stereotype people because of their race or religion, so, too, do we stereotype people because of their region of birth. All three types of stereotypes are wrong and equally unfair.

The great moral issues involved in the civil-rights struggle today are not different from those of 1948. I was Mayor of Minneapolis then and a delegate to the Democratic National Convention at Philadelphia. The speech I made at that time, supporting the civil-rights amendment to the party platform, was not without effect. That was the year when the Democratic Party did adopt a strong civil-rights plank, when Harry Truman won his magnificent victory over an array of opponents that included Thomas Dewey, Henry Wallace, and those Democrats who had walked out to organize the States' Rights Party. I have made considerably more than a thousand speeches since that day — July 14, 1948 — but this speech is one I recall with particular feeling. Here are some excerpts:

> . . . This proposal is made with no single region, no single class, no single
> racial or religious group in mind. All regions and all states have shared in the
> precious heritage of American freedom. All states and regions have at least some
> infringements of that freedom. All people, all groups, have been the victims of
> discrimination . . . We are here as Democrats. But more important, as Americans — and I firmly believe that as men concerned with our country's future, we must specify in our

platform the guarantees which I have mentioned.
Every citizen has a stake in the emergence of the United States as the leader of the free world. For us to play our part effectively, we must be in a morally sound position. Our demands for democratic practices in other lands will be no more effective than the guarantees of those practiced in our own country.

We place our faith in the brotherhood of man under the fatherhood of God.
There can be no compromise of the guarantees of civil rights. There can be no hedging, no watering down. There are those who say, we are rushing this issue of civil rights.
I say we are 172 years too late. There are those who say, this issue of civil rights is an infringement on states' rights. The time has arrived for the Democratic Party to get out of the shadow of states' rights and walk forthrightly into the bright sunshine of human rights. People — human beings — this is the issue of the twentieth century. People, all kinds and sorts of people, look to America for leadership.

I ask you for a calm consideration of our historic opportunity. Let us forget the evil passions, the blindness of the past. For all of us here, for the millions who have sent us, for the whole two billion members of the human family, our land is now, more than ever, the last best hope on earth. I know that we shall begin here the fuller, richer

realization of that hope, that promise of a land
where all men are free and equal, and
each man uses his freedom and equality wisely
and well.

I have expressed these thoughts in different versions, different words, quite a few times since — most recently when formal Senate debate began on the 1964 civil-rights bill. It is my way of saying, "Freedom now? Of course, in every possible way." I have heard Negroes, in their anguish, compare Nazi Germany at the time it was persecuting and killing millions with the United States today. The notion is remote to most Americans, and indeed, the equation cannot be made. Freedom riders symbolize the direction we are taking; the secret police symbolized theirs. All the forces of our Federal Government, our law, the will of the majority, and our common heritage are on the side of progress; in Nazi Germany, the course was one of constant downward spiral, into the pit of evil. But the mood of many Negroes is that they have long been condemned to a particular type of hell and that "gradualism" — in their eyes, gradual release from purgatory — is not the answer. Freedom is late enough in coming; how can anyone deny "Freedom now"?

It is imperative that we reassure our Negro citizens — and all the underprivileged, deprived, and discriminated against — that the liberal tradition is on their side and is powerful. We have the laws and we have the machinery for fighting prejudice — the hundreds of human-rights agencies and councils, public and private, throughout the United States. They need to be strengthened and encouraged. But what is needed most is for each man to live according to the precepts of his faith, to proclaim and daily act out his belief in the fifth freedom — respect for the dignity of all men.

IV

The Needs of Life

We are living in an age when America seems to be bursting with issues and problems. We must secure civil rights for all our citizens. We must end poverty. Our economy must grow in all parts of the country. Automation and technology must create new jobs, not more jobless. Old age must be welcomed with serenity and lived in dignity. We must rebuild our cities, revitalize our rural areas. We must provide wholesome leisure activity and recreation. We must conserve our national resources.

How could we have let all these problems accumulate? Where was our vision, our planning for the future? It is easy to denounce the sins of the past. But it is also futile to do so. Complaint and denunciation alone are never satisfactory; positive advocacy and action are needed to attain our goals. Besides, our problems today are not so much reflections of past failures as they are indications of the needs of progress. Let us not call them problems; let us call them challenges.

The material needs of life are dependent on the state of our complex economic system. It is a system that Marx could not have anticipated and that today's Communists — whether partisan to Khrushchev or to Mao — fail to understand. They have long waited for our economy to falter and fail. They say that we must preach war because our economy cannot prosper in peacetime. They are wrong. We seek peace — and we know that our economy, with proper planning, can meet all challenges. They will have to wait forever if they think their system can bury us. The American economic republic is the remarkable achievement of free men working together in a political democracy. The protection of freedom is the ultimate guarantee of progress. The results in our times have made the nineteenth-century achievements of the free market seem absolutely puny — and they make obsolete the Communist idea of state monopoly of economic power. Ours is the progressive system of the future; the Communists are the reactionaries.

Using Our Human Resources

Back in 1922, Sinclair Lewis added a word to our language in his novel about a "typical"

American, a neighbor we recognized then and still know today. Here is a passage from *Babbitt*: "The strikers had announced a parade for Tuesday morning . . . When Babbitt drove west from his office at ten that morning, he saw a drive of shabby men heading toward the tangled, dirty district beyond Court House Square. He hated them because they were poor, because they made him feel insecure. 'Damn loafers! Wouldn't be common workmen if they had any pep,' he complained."

George Babbitt, the book makes clear, was really a better and kinder man than he usually sounded. So, too, are many other men who make such statements about the poor and the unemployed. "Pep" may still be a virtue, but it is hardly the decisive factor in a man's condition of employment. The unemployed are not unemployed because they want to be; nor are the poor on relief because they want to be.

The single most important economic question facing the nation today — an issue that President Johnson has made abundantly clear in his call for a war on poverty — is whether the United States can achieve and maintain full employment and full utilization of our productive capacity. It is astonishing that we are the only major power with such a high rate of unemployment, such waste of our human resources. This nation, the epitome of free enterprise, the center of world capitalism, continues to tolerate over 5 per cent of its work force unemployed and more than 16 per cent of its plant capacity unused. It is astonishing because our over-all economic strength is wonderfully impressive.

When President Kennedy took office, early in 1961, we were in the midst of the third recession to hit the American economy in seven years. Nearly 7 per cent of the labor force were then unemployed; over 20 per cent of our manufacturing capacity lay idle. Actual output was running $50 billion behind the economy's potential. It appeared not only that recessions were inevitable, but that they were to become the rule rather than the exception.

Since then, the rate of activity in the United States economy has moved up sharply. Gross national product is up $100 billion, or 16 per cent, in constant dollars. Industrial production is up 23 per cent. Corporate profits before taxes are up $17 billion, or 44 per cent. The net income per farm for 1963 was up almost $375, or 12 per cent. Total after-taxes income of the American people is up $56 billion, or 16 per cent. Real disposable income per family is up more than $600, or 8 per cent.

An unparalleled peacetime record of rise in total output. And yet . . .

More than 4 million workers cannot find employment. The unemployment rate has not been below 5 per cent in over six years — and our labor force will expand at a much faster rate in the coming decade.

And one-fifth of our fellow citizens — 36 million Americans — live in poverty, below minimum standards of decency, with little hope.

The fault is not lack of Babbitt's "pep," but lack of the education, health, skills, jobs, and community and area resources that the other four-fifths of our nation enjoy. Clearly, we have much unfinished business.

The tax cut of early 1964 is clearly emerging as a major factor for economic expansion — an absolute necessity if we are to bring to a halt the intolerable waste of human resources. The tax cut should also help safeguard us against a recession that could have cost a minimum of $25 billion in lost output, perhaps an additional 2 million persons unemployed, and a severe setback in the advance toward our economic goals.

The main provisions of the tax bill were aimed at cutting individual income-tax collection by $8.8 billion and corporate tax liabilities by $1.5 billion in 1964. These reductions should pay for themselves many times over in increased jobs, output, consumption, and investment.

There are those who say that we must choose between efficiency and frugality in government on the one hand, and large Federal expenditures and debts to finance our unmet needs on the other. They also say that we must choose between maintaining an adequate defense posture and providing improved standards of health, education, and welfare for all our people.

I think that by now President Johnson and his administration have demonstrated that through judicious planning, these harsh, invidious choices can be avoided. While expanding vital programs in the areas of health, education, manpower training, retraining, urban renewal, and public housing, we can also fully satisfy our defense requirements.

Planning for greater employment of our human resources remains one of the greatest tasks ahead. For example, the United States must create 300,000 new jobs every month to keep up with new workers entering the labor force and older workers who have lost their jobs because of automation. By 1970, we must have created 35 million new jobs.

Technological progress is, of course, mainly responsible for the quickly changing patterns of our economic and employment situation. The changes that took place in American agriculture during the past century gave us a preview of today's challenge. In 1870, one farm worker produced enough food for five and a half persons; in 1940, a farm worker produced enough to feed ten and a half persons; today, one farm worker produces enough for twenty-seven persons.

The effects of this technological change are both good and bad. It costs considerably less now to produce the food we need than it did in 1940. But today, more than 200,000 men and women leave farms each year for lack of work, and agricultural workers constitute only about 8 per cent of our population. And, while farm incomes have improved substantially in the past three years, they still average only 60 per cent of nonfarm incomes.

As one way of coping with these and related

problems, early in 1964 I introduced legilation for the establishment of a Commission on Automation, Technology, and Employment. This was in line with a major proposal in President Johnson's State of the Union Message made at that time. It is obvious that automation and technology will have even greater effect on our society in years to come. In the President's words, "If we have the brainpower to invent these machines, we ought to have the brainpower to make certain they are a boon, not a bane, to humanity."

The legislation was introduced on the following grounds:

1) We must determine how we are going to translate new scientific knowledge gained in our military and aerospace research into civilian products for general use. Whole new industries could be created this way.

2) It is becoming consistent with our defense needs to cut down on the number of military personnel and uranium-producing processes, and to close obsolete bases. But arms reduction must not be allowed to result in increased unemployment or a reduced gross national product.

3) A whole new "systems approach" to large-scale problems has been developed in government-sponsored research. This involves cooperation among highly expert people in many disciplines. We must seek to adapt their skills and methods for application to the major problems of

the nation — in regional development, city planning, transportation, air and water pollution, and more. There is no reason to assume, for example, that the population drift to great cities hugging the coastline of America is inevitable, while the heartland of America is being drained of people.

I believe that such a commission would demonstrate that we do have enough knowledge to do creative regional planning to broaden the base of economic power in all parts of the country, to preserve the virtues of small and medium-sized community living, and to maintain the balance of regional vitality and strength in our nation.

The comprehensive bill I submitted, along with Senator Hart of Michigan, incorporates some of the proposals made in various earlier bills by some of my colleagues. Its purpose in calling for a Hoover-type commission is to draw from the expertise we have in both public and private sectors of the economy. The ability to solve our problems does not lie exclusively within the executive agencies or Congress. State and local government, as well as labor and management, can participate in attacking the problems and in defining and meeting community and human needs. The commission would recommend what each of these segments of society could do and how to do it most effectively.

The commission would be authorized to establish advisory panels of persons of exceptional competence and experience in the fields of science and technology, economics, political science, operations analysis, and business to develop relevant knowledge in each area. It would also explore means for principal defense contractors to initiate a continuing series of studies to develop plans for reconversion and diversification of current defense contracts and expenditures.

The other principal objectives of the legislation are:

1) To identify the major types of prospective technological and economic changes that are likely to occur and to aid in an understanding of their effect upon employment requirements.

2) To report on suitable policies for economic conversion resulting from reduction or changes in defense spending.

3) To report on the pace of technological change, its impact on productivity, its incidence among particular occupations and groups of workers, and its other effects upon the economy, communities, families, social structure, and human values.

4) To determine the relationship between the general level of unemployment and that produced by technological progress, and the best ways to bring about the speedy re-employment of workers displaced by automation and other forms of economic change.

5) To examine recent technological developments — particularly those resulting from

the Federal research and development program — in order to discover the most promising areas for new work.

In short, the Commission would be a means for harnessing some of our brain power.

At this point, we know that technological change accounts for about half the annual rate of our economic growth and has radically altered the income patterns of our economy. The agricultural component of our gross national product is only half of what it was three decades ago. The composition and characteristics of our labor force have been altered. Whole regional economies have been drastically affected. And many areas find themselves bypassed by technical change, relying still on natural resources, for which there is diminishing demand, or on the conversion of materials, which now requires fewer workers. The prosperity of any one region of the United States is no longer tied to abundant resources of mine or field or forest. Knowledge as a human resource is highly mobile and flexible. It is not unusual to see bursting prosperity in localities that have, substantially, only one product to sell — know-how.

If we accept the thesis that economic strength depends on technical ability, it is disturbing to compare the rate and direction of our technical effort with that of other nations. For example, the nations of Western Europe (including the U.K.), with their much smaller gross national products, sustain a "technical effort" to enhance private industry that is at least as great as that of the United States.

Moreover, this effort is being stepped up. In France, Germany, and England, nonspace, nonmilitary technical efforts have been doubling approximately every three to four years. The French research and development effort is expected to double again over the next four years and to exceed the United States research and development effort as a percentage of gross national product. In contrast, our own increase has been only a few percentage points per year. In fact, we have a diminishing rate of increase. In Italy, Belgium, the Netherlands, Norway, and Sweden, civilian research and much development amounts to 100 per cent of the total research and development effort. West Germany, which has the largest civilian research and development program, allocated in 1959 (the last year for which I have comparable figures) a total of $690 million for civilian research and development — which was 95 per cent of the total West German research and development effort. Two-thirds of France's research and development was civilian-oriented, as was about half of the United Kingdom's.

In contrast, for the same year, U.S. civilian research and development constituted only one-third of our total research and development effort.

The European developments (and Japanese, too) — the greater rate of economic growth and the greater emphasis on industry-oriented technology — bear directly on two major U.S. problems: We are in an increasingly stiff competition for world markets, and our balance of international payments continues to be stubbornly unfavorable.

We have long counted on our technological superiority and our large domestic market to give us the needed edge in international competition. These advantages tended to offset lower labor costs abroad. But improved technology and the merged economic strength of the Common Market are invalidating some of the assumptions of the past. At the same time, the increasing cost of European labor is giving us a better competitive position.

We must expand our exports. We have simply failed to win our share of world markets for American products. We have not been export-conscious in the past. For almost two hundred years we have enjoyed an economic honeymoon of sorts, with the demands of our own steadily increasing population keeping pace with our growing productive capacity. And we have, in a sense, allowed a great part of our potential productivity to sit in a warehouse, just waiting for foreign customers to come flocking to the door.

Our productive capacity is ahead of our domestic consumption capacity. What should be our triumphs have become our embarrassments. Agriculture is our greatest success story in production — but we tend to be ashamed of our surplus foods and fibers and jam them into storage bins. We have built great factories and plants — and now hundreds of them stand idle.

Increasing our exports will help solve the problem. Exports now account for only 4 per cent of our gross national product. The six countries of the European Common Market export 12 per cent of theirs — three times our rate. Other countries do even better.

We are supposed to be the best salesmen in the world. It would be good if we put that salesmanship to the test in foreign markets. The Federal Government has sought to encourage greater export activity. The trade program approved by Congress in 1962 provided the President with some tools to build up exports. New tax credits for investment should also encourage industry to invest in the new equipment and machinery needed to make the products suitable for foreign markets. Through the Export-Import Bank and the Foreign Credit Insurance Corporation, we have taken steps to improve credit availability and export insurance for commerical and political risks, so that American businessmen can compete with foreign exporters. And the government, primarily the Department of Commerce, has increased its efforts to send our products abroad, through creation of the National Export Expansion Council and by sending trade missions all over and participating in trade centers and fairs. But the real export job, selling our products, must still be done by private business.

Our past economic success has resulted, in large

measure, from our ability to adapt to the needs of changing times. To increase our exports, we know that we must improve the quality of our goods and reduce costs, direct and indirect. What must be done, therefore, is to broaden the technical base of our economy.

This can be achieved primarily through research and development. We now have an enormous research and development effort; in the past twenty years, our expenditures in this area have jumped from $500 million a year to over $16 billion.

But three-quarters of that enormous national technical effort is "Federally sponsored" for such purposes as defense, space, atomic energy, and public health — all vital national objectives, but none directed particularly toward promoting civilian economic growth. Indeed, the results of this increasingly esoteric research have less and less immediate application to the civilian economy.

Only about $4 billion is spent annually by industry for industry research, and of that amount, only about $1.5 billion is aimed at increasing productivity. Although industry-sponsored research has grown in the last several years, the rate of increase has been significantly slower than that of government-sponsored work. Last year it barely increased at all.

Moreover, 80 per cent of this industry-sponsored research was done in 300 companies; 73 per cent was concentrated in 5 industries; and 2 of these industries — aerospace and electronics — accounted for more than 25 per cent of the research and development, although they constituted only 10 per cent of the manufacturing component of the gross national product.

On the other hand, such industries as building and construction, textiles and apparel, and food processing — which made up about 30 per cent of the manufacturing and construction components of the gross national product — accounted for less than 4 per cent of privately supported research and development.

The 50 per cent growth of industrial research and development in the last decade has taken place in large firms almost exclusively. Firms with more than 5,000 employees increased research and development 50 per cent, whereas smaller firms increased it about 2 per cent.

This concentration of research and development in certain industries and in large firms has special significance, because there is a high and direct correlation between growth and profitability and the relative amount of research and development performed.

The growth of military and space research has further concentrated technical effort in firms and areas already technically competent. Almost half the total military research and development (46 per cent) is now concentrated on the West Coast; the Middle Atlantic states account for almost a fifth; and of the remaining third, the South has about 9.5 per cent, the mountain states almost 9 per cent, and the Midwest 8 per cent.

A similar pattern is clear in the geographic distribution of trained human resources — specifically, scientists and engineers. In 1960, the number of engineers per million population was 3,330 in the South — roughly half the number on the West Coast, 6,570. The Midwest, with 4,580 engineers per million population, was also sharply below the West and East coasts.

In 1961, the number of scientists per million population was 750 in the Midwest, compared with 1,240 on the West Coast and about 1,035 per million in the New England-Middle Atlantic region. The Midwest has become a net exporter of scientists and engineers to both coasts. Our Midwestern universities are training men and women who are migrating in increasing numbers out of the region. State money is being used, in a very real sense, to provide advanced-degree training for out-of-state industry. If there were a two-way flow of advanced-degree graduates back into the Midwest from the West and East coasts, this would be a tolerable situation. But the Federal procurement dollar is providing the overwhelming majority of job opportunities in limited areas of our country, and that is where the flow of trained people goes. I believe that a conscious effort should be made on the part of the Federal Government to break this pattern by a wider distribution of government procurement.

Another example of this kind of imbalance in research and development activities is the fact that, out of 2,000 universities in the United

States, 100 of them, or 5 per cent, perform 90 per cent of Federally supported academic research.

A serious by-product of the present research and development pattern is that university faculty and students tend to commit themselves to technical activity suited to space, defense, and similar missions — instead of to the more mundane, less glamorous, but vital mission of increasing economic productivity and developing new products. Such a bias in the career orientation of our brightest minds is perhaps the most disturbing problem arising out of the necessary but heavy concentration on special national-security programs.

Of the 400,000 scientists and engineers in the United States doing research and development, about 275,000 are performing their work for government programs, and only the remaining 125,000 for industry-oriented programs. But of this industry group, about 100,000 work for the 300 large companies that account for the bulk of industrial research and development activities; the remaining 25,000 are scattered among all the other industrial and commercial enterprises in America.

The increase in the supply of scientists and engineer for research and development during 1963 amounted to about 30,000. But the increase in space research and development alone in 1964 will absorb just about the entire new supply. The number of scientists and engineers needed for this space increase will be equivalent to more than 20 per cent of the total now doing research and development for the private sector, and to about 50 per cent of the research and development people in universities.

And things are going to get worse. By 1970, we can expect to be short by more than 250,000 engineers. Enrollments in engineering in American schools have actually declined; we are graduating about 30,000 engineers each year now, while the Russians are graduating 120,000 yearly.

It is my view that trained, educated people constitute our major natural resource. And this natural resource deserves national support. By that, I mean Federal support — as I shall explain in the section on youth and education.

We have recognized this in principle, but we have taken only relatively small and cautious steps — for instance, the National Defense Education Act — to implement the idea.

The cold fact is that the number of engineering graduates is declining — as are Ph.D.'s in education and government. We cannot permit this to continue.

Neither can we afford to permit the continued and accelerating concentration of our most talented young people in almost purely defense-oriented industry, without risking intellectural starvation of the civilian-oriented sector of our society.

The worsening supply and demand situation in trained manpower is only one of the serious limitations on an expanded development and use of technology for industry and commerce. There are others — including the rising costs of the many operations connected with the introduction of new products and processes, and the increasing risks involved in innovation.

Such limitations do not permit industry alone, as matters now stand, to achieve the level of technical effort necessary to increase our economic growth rate to a minimum of 4.5 per cent yearly and to increase our exports.

The Federal Government has traditionally contributed significantly to the advancement of science and technology for nonmilitary, nonspace activities in several specialized areas. The major areas included: atomic energy ($230 million); agriculture ($176 million); basic science ($153 million); transportation — mostly air ($121 million); and natural resources ($107 million).

We have an important stake in the well-being of industry and commerce, just as we have in agriculture, fisheries, mining, transportation, forests, public health, or space exploration and defense. We must encourage more interaction between specialists in science and technology, economics, and related fields. We must encourage industry-oriented basic research at universities, and increase the supply of technical people knowledgeable about industrial problems. We must seek additional support by industry itself of basic technical work.

By stimulating basic technological development that will have a major effect on industrial productivity, we will be able to contribute significantly to our gross national product, reduce the indirect costs of goods and services, and expand our export trade.

I should say, parenthetically, that I believe that we are victims of several myths about our economy. Those who are relatively tight with money and credit tend to consider as expenditures many things that are really assets. A hydroelectric dam is too often charged off as an expenditure, not an asset. Farmers Home Administration loans, with their fairly high rates of interest, are often rated as expenditures. Yet they make money for the government. I believe our budgetary methods are unrelated to the realities of modern society. (Sweden and Germany, for example, have more modern systems.) It is far more possible for us to "save" ourselves into a depression than it is to spend ourselves into one, although wasteful, purposeless spending can seriously damage our economy. A small degree of inflation has inevitably accompanied an expanding economy. Deflation, to any degree, is ominous. My point is that we should make much more credit available if the economy is to flourish, and we must think in terms of purposeful, constructive investment, as does any sound business planner.

Another myth is that our economy has been hurt by labor strikes. We are putting our unemployed into economic ghettoes, and yet we protest the damage done by strikes. We would do well to be far more indignant over unemployment than we are; the nation has lost fewer man-hours through strikes and lockouts in the past thirty-five years than it loses through unemployment in just one year.

Above all, we must realize that we cannot solve the specific problems caused by automation, conversion from military production, competitive international trade, and other economic trends without a massive upgrading of our human resources. We need to put more of our intellectual capital into solving these problems. We need to create more intellectual capital by moving faster at the task of training, retraining, and extending the benefits of higher education at a time when the need for and function of unskilled workers are dropping sharply.

That will be our new strength — more educated and skilled workers, more citizens who are trained to take advantage of and contribute to an America revolutionized by technology. It will be our way of ending the blight of poverty that haunts this richest of nations. It will be very real, very vital evidence of our "pep" — non-Babbitt style.

Big Business and Labor

Two of the mainstays of our remarkable economic system also seem to be two of our pet scapegoats — big business and organized labor.

"Bigness," per se, can be bad — and I have made my criticisms of it. Big business can be "bad" when it stifles competition and blocks expansion. It is "good" when it helps us to achieve ever-rising standards of living.

The conservative, who somehow never minds bigness in business, often criticizes bigness in labor and, most certainly, the big or mass aspects of public planning. He opposes Medicare, public housing, mass transit, farm subsidies, and Federal grants-in-aid. He talks of the "evil reaches of government power which curb our freedom." He forgets that hunger curtails freedom in harsher, and more real ways than any imagined curbs produced by government planning. Poverty curtails individual freedom. So do illiteracy, prejudice, lack of education, inability to obtain the basic needs of life.

I do not think that we have many real grievances to be urged against bigness in business today. To the contrary. For the most part, big corporations are a source of strength and economic vitality. And certainly, big business is here to stay.

Some Americans hark back to the days before the managerial revolution, back to the days of the "robber barons." But this country and its economy have matured spectacularly since the trust-busting days of Theodore Roosevelt, William Howard Taft, and Woodrow Wilson. And business has changed along with other institutions.

This is not to minimize the evils of the past. The U.S. Supreme Court, in a landmark decision exploring the reasons for the enactment of the Sherman Antitrust Act in 1890, gave an idea of the inequities of the past:

The main cause which led to the legislation was

> the thought that it was required
> by the economic conditions of the times, that is, the vast accumulation of wealth
> in the hands of corporations and individuals, the enormous development of corproate
> organizations, the facility for combination which such organizations afforded,
> the fact that the facility was being used, and that combinations known as trusts
> were being multiplied, and the widespread impression that their power had been and would be exerted to oppress individuals and injure the public generally.

The tendency to attack "bigness" as such stems from our proper concern that monopoly shall not stifle the operation of our competitive society. The big businesses of bygone generations did, indeed, act in a pattern of savage repression of competition. And current revelations of price-fixing and other price-holding practices do not help to ease a strong historical suspicion of the motives of great corporations on the part of government leaders, small businessmen, and others.

Does big business by its very size tend to smother competition, make production less efficient, and accumulate undue political power? Does big business actually profit through more efficiently produced goods at lower prices, or because industrial giants can hold prices artificially higher than true competition would permit? The answers to these questions are not easy.

First of all, the pluralistic economy of the 1960's bears little resemblance to the economy of the turn of the century that brought forth the first great trust-busting wave. Everything about our economy is on a vaster scale today. The gross national product (after allowing for the decreased value of the dollar) is more than six times as large as it was at the opening of the century. A "big business" in Wilson's time was a corporation owning $500 million in assets. Today, one corporation alone owns $24.6 billion, and there are a number whose assets top $5 billion; 2,200 American companies own more than $50 million in assets.

Yet big business does not, in fact, dominate our economy. The 100 largest industrial companies account for only 10 per cent of the sales of all industrial, commercial, and agricultural enterprises. And, surprisingly, the total share of "big business" in our economy does not appear to be increasing over the long haul.

There are almost 5 million American business firms with paid employees. If you include farms, we have about 9 million sole proprietors and more than 2 million partners. Such figures demonstrate how radically distorted is the Communist concept of an economy marching to the tune of a handful of capitalists.

Ownership of American corporations is far more widely spread than at the turn of the century. Today, it is rare for one or two individuals to "own" a great corporation.

American Telephone and Telegraph acquired its 2-millionth stockholder in 1961, and the largest "owner" has only a fraction of 1 per cent. Corporate stock ownership is distributed among almost 15 million Americans, although, of course, the effective control of a corporation can be exercised through the leverage of a relatively few individuals.

Large firms play a major role in our economy in many respects. They conduct the great bulk of the privately financed research. Basic research facilities of two of our largest companies — General Electric and AT&T's Bell Laboratories — rank among the world's top scientific institutions. Management teams of some of these great industrial conglomerations are capable of fantastic achievements. In World War II, General Motors produced one-fourth of all our airplane engines, tanks and armored cars; almost half of all our machine guns and carbines; two-thirds of all heavy trucks; and three-fourths of all the Navy's diesel-engine horsepower. Ford's application of assembly-line mass production to aircraft at Willow Run produced 8,600 Liberator bombers. Ford also produced 57,000 aircraft engines, 27,000 tank engines, 278,000 jeeps, 13,000 amphibious jeeps, and 92,000 trucks, plus numbers of gliders, tanks, and AA directors.

When Du Pont was asked by the government to take on mass production of plutonium — to beat the Nazis to the atomic bomb — management responded magnificently. Equipment never before imagined had to be designed and built, thousands of workers recruited and trained. There were no guideposts. There was no experience. But Du Pont did it, and the United States made the first atomic bomb within three years.

Unquestionably, alert, experienced industrial management teams must be considered one of the most critical assets of our nation in peace as well as war.

Indeed, it is high time that the traditional hostility between the intellectuals on the one hand and management on the other was ended. Doctrinaire thinking has no place in the vital and proliferating society of the 1960's. Frankly, the country needs the *joint* thinking of the finest minds in business and of the best men and women we have in government, education, labor, and the great voluntary organizations. What is needed is a sense of overriding national purpose which calls men to rise above their daily concerns with making a living, getting ahead of the competition, or expanding their sphere of influence. The challenge of political leadership is the enlistment of our best people across the board, economically and socially, in the solving of national problems and the planning of national programs.

Bigness is here to stay in this expanding economy. Depending on the levels of research and technology, the optimum size for a corporation in a given industry may range from small to middle-sized to very large. The Antitrust Division of the Justice Department raises its eyebrows when mergers and acquisitions begin building into a size and structure that go beyond efficiency and thrust into the area of probable restraint of competition.

I would prefer to add a subtitle to the Antitrust Division — "pro-competitive." Our goal is an environment within which all types of business rivalry can flourish. We do not want to limit the growth of those large firms whose efficiency can mean better and cheaper products to consumers.

The chief internal economic role of government must be the smoothing of the way for new men and new ideas. Where lack of credit stifles growth, government should see that it is provided. When patent rights are being used to foster monopoly, rather than reward inventive skill, government should insist on other companies' being allowed to use patents on reasonable terms. When the power of large corporations is misused to restrain competition, the Antitrust Division must act swiftly and decisively.

The most successful preventive to monopoly has been and continues to be growth of markets. Our growing U.S. market, with the vigorous pressure of new ideas arising from research technology, and a steady encouragement to smaller businesses over the past several decades, has given us the benefits of very large business enterprises, without a fatal development of monopolistic behavior.

Big business is a fundamental part of our economic life. And most certainly, organized labor is, too. Many economists, political scientists, and philosophers have written at length about the basic meaning and goals of trade unionism. I think that Hillel, the Hebrew sage, expressed it best centuries ago in one brief comment: "If I am not for myself, who will be for me. But if I am only for myself, what am I?"

This is the real story of American labor. Working men and women have banded together to further their mutual interests. If they failed to do it for themselves, who would do it for them? But they could not be concerned with their problems alone. If they were only for themselves, what were they?

It is a tragic fact that the disclosures of Congressional committees and newspapers are mainly limited to what is wrong with American labor. The story of a $100 bribe to a labor racketeer appears far more newsworthy than the story of a $10,000 contribution by a union to a philanthropic cause. I am not saying that strikes and violence and labor corruption are not worthy of public attention. I think we should all be informed about the issues in a strike, why violence results, which union officials have violated their trust.

But we should also know the full story of what decent, honorable, devoted trade-unionists are doing day by day for their fellow men, for their country, and for the cause of freedom.

Union organizations have provided for millions of formerly inarticulate citizens the forum in which to hammer out policies affecting the world in which they live and which their children will inherit. And not only have they hammered out policies, but they have developed techniques and resources for implementing those policies. That is what I find so right about the labor movement. Unions have made democracy and citizenship and the right to petition a reality to millions of men and women.

Perhaps the most stimulating periods I ever spend are the 20- and 30-minute sessions I have with groups of textile workers, rubber workers, and communication workers who come to Washington to attend their unions' legislative institutes. I doubt whether I knew what debate really was until I had to answer the searching, down-to-earth questions put to me by workers who knew from firsthand experience the problems of automation, of unemployment, of old age, of radiation hazards, of slums.

The unions have given their people a voice. That is one thing right about the labor movement.

Some years ago, I shared a platform with William Schnitzler, Secretary-Treasurer of the AFL-CIO. In the audience were many dozens of union officials and technicians involved in the vital work of administering health plans, union hospitals, and medical centers, working together with some of the nation's leading medical and insurance authorities. This was nothing new to me — finding union representatives actively involved with other groups in seeking solutions to America's challenges.

Mr. Schnitzler made an eloquent plea for bringing full medical care within the reach of all American families. He spoke forthrightly about labor's right and its responsibility to speak out on this issue on behalf of all Americans. In doing so, he explained simply and effectively American labor's role in the whole area of legislation and community activites:

> I find it rather amusing — but also distressing — that labor is sometimes attacked, on the one hand, for being a selfish vested interest, and then, on the other hand — by the very same critics — for injecting itself into issues that are not related only to trade unions and their members, and presuming to speak for underprivileged, unorganized workers.
>
> American labor does presume to speak for more than its own membership. It does this partially as a matter of simple enlightened self-interest. We believe that what is good for America is good for American labor. In one area after another, it is clear that our own members will improve their lot in life only as all the people in the community improve theirs. There is a limit to the things we can obtain for our own members at the collective bargaining table, although we have by no means reached that limit. The welfare, happiness, and security of our people

require sound legislation. They also require the development of appropriate cooperative and other forms of voluntary organizations designed to promote the general welfare. In all of these aspects of American life, the labor movement plays a constructive role. The fact of the matter is that there is no really articulate voice of the people. The closest thing to it is the labor movement. We are happy and proud to serve as a people's lobby. We represent at least 50 million men, women, and children in the families of our members. But in much of our work in Congress, in the state legislatures, in the school systems, in the voluntary organizations — we sincerely believe we speak out for the great bulk of all Americans.

For a hundred years now, no one has worked more vigorously than American labor for free, universal education.

There has been no group more active in seeking improvements in our social-security laws.

Although few of our own members qualify, we have fought hard for public housing because we know that slums are incompatible with our free America.

In making these observations, I don't mean to suggest that we have done these things by ourselves. In every one of these activities, we have always been associated with others — groups like those represented at this conference. But we do say proudly that American labor has tried for all these years to use its organized strength in the pursuit of the general welfare.

As a Senator, I can give personal testimony as to what American labor seeks from the Congress of the United States. Labor lobbyists are not coy in expressing labor's goals. Of course, they seek legislation that will permit them to organize and to function with a minimum of government interference. But labor-relations legislation is only a small part of their legislative program — albeit a very important part.

Labor long asked that the Federal minimum wage be increased and that its coverage be expanded. Very few union members need a Federal minimum wage to protect them. Is this narrow, self-interest legislation?

Labor asks for improvement in unemployment insurance. Union members would benefit from this, but there are a greater number of nonunion workers who need this additional protection. A growing number of union workers, as a matter of fact, look to union-negotiated supplementary unemployment insurance for their own protection. Do not all wage earners in the nation deserve adequate protection against the hazards of unemployment?

Labor asks for health benefits for retired people. It asks for higher appropriations for medical reserach and hospitals and child-welfare activities. Labor lobbies for public housing and slum clearance and urban redevelopment.

Labor seeks depressed-areas legislation, help for

community facilities, bigger public roads programs.

Labor supports Federal aid to school construction, better salaries for teachers, liberal scholarship programs.

Labor favors multipurpose river projects and atomic-energy development for peaceful purposes and conservation of our natural resources.

Labor supports programs designed to aid America's farmers, such as REA, and it backs legislation to preserve the family-size farm.

Labor favors legislation designed to promote a vigorous and healthy climate for small business.

Labor is a strong backer of civil-rights legislation, despite the difficulties such support causes in some parts of the country.

These are all valid social goals. They are not sought by labor out of narrow self-interest.

But labor looks beyond even this. It would be understandable if American labor, troubled as it is with its own problems of unemployment and automation, stayed out of international affairs. It could, as it once did, fight to keep all immigrants from our shores and to get protectionist tariffs on all imports. It could oppose mutual security and technical assistance and insist that America's own underdeveloped and depressed areas receive these billions of dollars of assistance. But American labor, for the most part, understands the external threats — both direct and indirect — to our security.

Organized labor's role in stemming Communism and helping the less-developed areas of the world is a magnificent story, still to be told fully. History will glorify the part Philip Murray played in this significant democratic victory. American labor has supported vital projects in Latin America, in the Middle East, in Hong Kong, in India — wherever there are human problems crying out for help. The plight of the world's refugees has received special consideration from American labor. Often the bulk of the aid comes not from union treasuries but from voluntary contributions by individual members. The leadership of George Meany in the international struggle for freedom is little known, but has been as effective and notewrothy as that of many generals and diplomats.

These truths must always be understood, the value of a free, honest labor movement remembered. Whenever we take steps to help the labor movement prevent or correct abuses which have crept into it, let us take great pains not to hurt the labor movement itself or to interfere with the progress it has made for all of us.

I like to be considered a friend of labor, just as I like to be considered pro-people, or pro-peace, or pro-free enterprise. And I think the cause of each is intertwined.

Walter Reuther once told me the story of a labor benefit we sometimes forget: An elderly worker came up to him after he had given a speech. "You know, Walter, everything you told us tonight is fine," the old man said in a thick Polish accent. "I know how much the union has done for me. You're right when you say it helped me get better wages, better hours, a pension, and seniority.

"But do you know what the union really means to me?" he continued. "Twenty years ago, when I first came to this shop, everybody called me 'dumb Polack.' Now they call me 'Brother.' "

The Apostle Paul once said it another way: "Be ye members one of another." That is what our unions have done for millions of men and women.

Agriculture: The Challenge of Abundance

Secretary of State Dean Rusk recently reminded us of one of our greatest assets: "The miracle of American agriculture has not merely produced more and more food for a still-hungry world," he said. "It has turned men's hopes toward science and technology and their appetites away from plunder and conquest. It has opened the historical possibility to meeting by peaceful means the elementary daily needs of the whole human race."

That miracle also has given us several challenges. One of them is how to convert this blessing of abundance into a benefit for the people who have made it possible — the American farmers.

Each year, the level of American agricultural production achieves new records, more than enough to meet the needs of domestic consumption and commercial exports. The American farmer will continue to outproduce his

Soviet counterpart year after year. The Soviet Union, which lacks the incentives fundamental to our family farm system, is waging a production war on its own soil. Ironically, Soviet agricultural failures are having a benign influence on world affairs by forcing a realignment of resources from armaments to fertilizers, thus effecting a degree of disarmament.

In a previous chapter, I noted that the changes which have taken place in agriculture in the past century have given us a preview of what we can expect from technological change in industry generally. One good effect is that it costs us far less to produce food than it did before. A bad effect is that, although farm income has improved substantially in the past three years, it still averages only 60 per cent of nonfarm income, with farm prices far below parity. This means that the farmer, to some extent, is subsidizing consumers.

The gallant 8 per cent of our population that takes the risks of drought, flood, hail, early frost, and insects also is subject to additional devastating risk: fluctuations and changes in domestic and world-wide markets. However, by any statistical measurement, the most distressing problem of all is the underemployment and low income in many rural areas.

For several years, we have had a program designed to lift some of the burden of poverty from the 15 million citizens living in rural areas. Of the 8 million families in the United States with incomes of less than $2,500 a year, more than half live in rural areas. More than one-fifth of the 22 million youths who live in rural areas are members of poverty families — and each year 200,000 more children are born into these families.

Despite all its problems, though, that 8 per cent of our population is able to produce the abundance that feeds and clothes us so well, that enables us to export $6 billion worth of farm products a year and still have plenty left over.

The technological revolution not only is irreversible (except for the effect of adverse weather), but also is accelerating at an enormous rate. One farmer now produces enough to feed twenty-seven people, while twenty years ago he produced only enough for eleven. Not only is the American consumer now enjoying his food at the lowest cost, in terms of human effort expended, of any people in the world; he also has the world's richest and most nutritious diet. Today, only about 19 per cent of the average consumer income is spent for food and fiber, compared with 27 per cent in 1947. This is the lowest percentage on record, and the lowest in the world relative to earnings. If Americans were eating the same diet as in the 1930's, the average family would budget only about 15 per cent of its earnings for food.

We also are eating better. We have witnessed a massive shift from cheaper carbohydrates, such as bread and potatoes, to the more expensive protein, high-vitamin foods, such as meat, milk, fruits, and vegetables. The housewife is getting better quality and more processing and precooking in the food she buys. Thus, the cost of food actually has declined even more than the above figures indicate.

Aside from farmers themselves, there are another 40 million people who make up our rural population, may of them engaged in small-town businesses. An additional 10 million people have jobs storing, transporting, processing, and merchandising the products of agriculture. Another 6 million help provide farmers' supplies.

Add them all up — the farmers, the small-town shopkeepers and bankers, the truckers, processors, wholesalers, and retailers — and we have close to 40 per cent of our population.

Still, we seem to take much of our agricultural industry for granted. We have saddled it with the accumulated legislation of the past thirty years, much of it now outmoded.

For example, our policies sometimes create the impression that the fruits of our farmers' labors are so great that they are liabilities. To imply, even remotely, that we are trying to get rid of "surpluses" in our export market is to downgrade the commodity in the eyes of those who might want to buy it. We have arrived at a stage where we can tell the world that our supplies of commodities, while available for sale, will be liquidated only at a certain level — and that such liquidation will be orderly. Farmers, and all the rest of us, need a sane reserve policy, based on facts, not on prejudice.

Americans generally, I fear, have not fully

understood the great contributions made by farmers to the well-being of the nation. There has been constant reiteration in the press and elsewhere of the difficulties arising from the costly acquisition and storage of a few commodities.

To help offset this, I introduced legislation in the first session of the Eighty-eighth Congress that would require Congress and the Department of Agriculture to establish national food and fiber reserves. These would be declared essential for our national security and safety and for the public health. Such a policy is long overdue. Until we have clearly identified what we mean by adequate reserves of food and fiber, there will be difficult and precarious market conditions affecting the prices of agricultural products. Too often people have made reserve stocks synonymous with surpluses. For many commodities, the total carryover stocks are entirely too low. We must be sure that food reserves are maintained at a level that will assure the continuation of a healthful standard of living, even in case of a serious setback. In the absence of such reserves, such a setback could set off a chain of inflationary forces, creating long-term economic difficulties.

Another problem constantly facing farmers is the possibility of a sharp drop in income unless wheat legislation is passed by the Congress when the present Act expires in 1965. The proposal for a wheat act, which I introduced in 1963, was the result of months of study and discussion with representatives of every farm organization and many leading farm economists.

Basically, my wheat bill represents a voluntary conservation program. It provides for $2 wheat in the domestic market and competitive prices for the world market. It would help us meet our needs at home and abroad. It would encourage proper use of the soil through conservation incentive payments to wheat growers. It would permit and encourage the farmer to use land taken out of wheat production for the planting of crops in short supply. It would thus provide a better income for the farmer, at less cost to taxpayers, and it would permit him to compete in world markets without violating any international agreements. The wheat bill ultimately passed in 1964 falls considerably short of providing a fair income to wheat farmers, but it does provide a program in which there can be some management of the problem of price-depressing surpluses.

The American farmer is, of course, vitally affected by all changes in world trading patterns. Here are some of the international facts that have great bearing on our agricultural policy and well-being:

The sudden and possibly continuing dependence of the Soviet Union and Eastern Europe on the free world for supplies of feed grains and wheat.

The European Economic Community's strenuous efforts to develop a cohesive agricultural policy.

The potential changes in policy related to agricultural imports in the European Free Trade Association, especially in the United Kingdom.

The expanding populations of Latin America, Asia, and Africa.

Let us examine the relationship of our farmers to our foreign policy and the ways they serve it.

While the quantity and quality of United States food consumption has increased, we also have seen a sharp increase in exports of food and fiber. We now export about $6 billion worth of food and fiber annually, of which about $4.2 billion is in sales for hard currency. In our balance-of-payment account, our total exports exceed total imports by about $2.4 billion. Thus our agricultural abundance is greatly aiding our balance-of-payments situation.

The simplest way to maintain our balance of payments is to utilize better the productive efficiency of our farmers by finding ways to increase our agricultural exports even more. The American farmer has a tremendous stake in the policies that are developed in the European Economic Community, because they have a vital bearing on what may happen to farm exports to the Common Market. Our government must do all it can to make sure that American farm exports are not handicapped by EEC agricultural policy. The opportunity to expand our farm exports is excellent if we bargain hard and from strength. The President has been given authority by Congress to negotiate for the opening of greater trade opportunities through the Trade Expansion Act. This authority will be used to attempt to gain tariff and other concessions in favor of our agricultural exports.

Here is one spectacular example of the export possibilities in the European Common Market area. The present total population of the EEC countries is about 175 million and is increasing at a steady rate. The wages of their workers are increasing rapidly. When wages of low-income groups go up, often the first use made of the extra income is to buy more meat. The average meat consumption in the European Economic Community increased from 101 pounds per person in 1955-56 to 118 pounds per person in 1960-61. As the meat consumption rises, so does the need for feed grains and protein meals.

If these people were to increase their meat consumption to the United States per capita level, their livestock would require imports of several times the current levels of feed grains and protein meals. This would provide a great opportunity for United States agriculture and industry to produce and to export. It would add to both farm income and nonfarm income, and at the same time provide substantial help to the balance of trade. I am convinced that this and other opportunities will be available in other parts of the world, if we are in a competitive position with other sellers. We must offer the best quality at the most reasonable price. There is no substitute for price and quality when it comes to competing for commercial markets abroad.

Under the Food for Peace program, established by Public Law 480 in 1955, food has become an important form of economic assistance to underdeveloped countries. It was our farmers' productive ability that made this effort possible.

Witness the following:

In the nine years that the Food for Peace program has been in existence, we have been able to ship overseas a grand total of almost $13 billion worth of food. During that same period, dollar sales amounted to $26 billion. Our food donations have been greatly increased in the past two or three years. They now provide supplemental feeding for 100 million undernourished people. Three-fourths of all the commodities are now programmed for children through organized school lunch efforts, through other nutritional feeding, and through family feeding plans in which the parents may participate by exchanging work for food.

One of the features of the Food for Peace program that has given me the greatest satisfaction has been the extension of school lunch programs to 40 million children in 91 countries. In many areas of the world, this Food for Peace school lunch is the only real meal the child gets all day; many children have been encouraged to go to school just to get that one meal. Educators in the affected areas have told me that the learning capacity of the children has been increased tremendously.

We have initiated a program under which we use food for wages. The food is used to pay for the building of roads and schools, the establishment of irrigation systems, the construction of homes and public buildings, and the settlement of new areas. Here we have a program under which the workers get food that is needed to feed their families at the same time that they work to better their communities.

American food is being used to provide a stabilizing force in many new emerging nations attempting to develop within a democratic framework.

As economic conditions permit, Food for Peace nations graduate to dollar markets. For example, Japan, not many years ago a beneficiary of the Food for Peace program, has become the largest single purchaser of American farm products. The Japanese have cultivated a taste for U.S. wheat, milk, vegetable oils, and corn products, a taste whetted by our Food for Peace donations, including the special school lunch program. Spain has become a $70 million a year cash market for United States farm products. Market development funds generated under Public Law 480 were used to build this demand. Some years ago, the soybean industry persuaded the Spanish Government to try some of our soybean oil under the Food for Peace program. Soon the foreign currency sales of soybean oil were replaced by dollar sales. Currently, Spain is a tremendous each buyer of our soybean oil.

When the history of the twentieth century is written, the development and expansion of the

Food for Peace program is sure to be viewed as one of the most constructive steps ever undertaken by any nation. Without our farmers' abundant productivity, this could not have been possible.

The Economic Research Service of the U.S. Department of Agriculture recently completed a significant study. The basic question raised was: "How can the world produce food for a population that will more than double, from 3 to 6 billion, in less than four decades?"

Diets have improved steadily in the so-called developed world. Today, there are no shortages of food on a nationwide basis anywhere in the West. However, there are food deficits almost everywhere in the less-developed parts of the world — Asia, Africa, and Latin America. There, populations have increased much more rapidly than food production, and the number of people suffering from malnutrition has actually increased since the early 1900's. In the years ahead, the less-developed regions will have great difficulty in providing more and more people with even the same low-quality diets.

In an era of new nations and rising aspirations, we must face this challenge. People want and need more and better food, with more of the proteins, fats. and other nutrients essential for normal health. The Economic Reserach Service study showed that, even with greatly expanded food imports, the less-developed areas of the world, in order to succeed in raising the available food per person 20 per cent above the present levels by the end of this century, would have to increase present food output by approximately as much as the current food production of the entire world. Despite their limited resources, they would have to achieve an annual increase in production rates for food substantially higher than that ever attained by the so-called affluent societies of North America and the rest of the industrial West.

In the world today, 4 children are born every second — well over 300,000 a day. Man has scarcely begun to assess the long-term implications of this phenomenal growth rate. The United Nations estimates that nearly 3.5 billion people will be added to the world population by the end of this century. Most of the people will be added in the less-developed countries, areas that are least able to feed themselves. By 2000 A.D., Asia alone will have a population greater than the present population of the entire world.

The less-developed world is carrying a double burden — a population growth twice that of the West with a much smaller per capita availability of land, water, and other natural resources. The "man-land" ratio is out of balance. Since not very much new land can be brought into production, the only escape valve in terms of food production is a higher yield per acre.

Prewar Asia was a net exporter of some 2 million metric tons of grain per year. By 1960-61, it was a net importer of 16 million metric tons of grain per year.

During the late 1930'd, Latin America was the dominant supplier of the world grain markets, exporting more grain than North America and

Oceania put together. By 1960-61, this area was importing grain both to feed a bigger population and to provide a somewhat better diet.

Africa was not traditionally much of a grain exporter of importer. Although Africa's grain output has kept pace with population growth, it has slipped over the line to become an importer of about 2 million metric tons of grain a year in order to meet its people's growing demands.

Western Europe has long been the world's largest grain market. However, as we have noted, the Soviet Union, which has been a net exporter of grain along with the rest of Eastern Europe, is developing a sizable deficit and may continue to need substantial imports.

This leaves North America and Oceania as the only major grain suppliers. It seems apparent that North America will become increasingly important as the supplier of grains to the world's deficit regions.

The solution to this world problem calls for a reappraisal of annual world food requirements and resources. Furthermore, we need to take a new look at world food reserves to meet the vagaries of weather. In recent years, the weather cycle struck down the grain crops of mainland China; the accumulated surpluses of North America and Oceania came to the rescue. In 1963, these accumulated surpluses were called upon to meet the reduced crop yield of the Soviet Union and Eastern Europe. By the end of the 1963-64 crop season, U.S.-government-held surplus stocks of food and feed grains were greatly reduced.

We are not certain how long the adverse weather cycle will hover over the Soviet Union and Eastern Europe. We do not know how soon the favorable crop years in North America may turn into years of substantially lower yields. It is at a moment such as this that we must do our best to foresee the future. We must not underestimate the importance of weather to crops. Louis M. Thompson, Associate Dean of Agriculture at Iowa State University, recently told a water-reserach symposium that "about half of the increase in yield [of grain crops] for 1950 to 1960 can be attributed to a change to more favorable weather, and only about half the upward trend was due to technology." And, he suggested, "a moving average for corn yield in Iowa describes a weather trend better than it describes a trend for adoption of technology."

We have many years of past meteorological study to help give us some insight into the future. We must utilize this as well as current research and study in order to be prepared.

Too often the whole matter of agricultural policy — with its tremendous importance to all the world — has been considered in political rather than economic terms, and thus the orientation has not been toward the real solution of problems. Too often we have been evading our responsibility with halfway and temporary measures.

There is basic need today for a high-level, bipartisan commission to examine the agricultural policy of this country. Its members should include representatives of such groups as farmers, consumers, businessmen, and the government. The task before it is fairly clear. Its function, essentially, is to evaluate properly the role of agriculture in the national and world economies. The following are some specific areas it should cover:

1) The efficient and effective marketing of farm products, with an emphasis on the interrelation of the diverse economic interests involved in the storage, transportation, processing, and merchandising of them.

2) Our trade relationships with European Economic Community, Latin American, Asian, and Soviet-bloc countries.

3) A comprehensive survey leading to suggestions for the solution of the increase in rural poverty and decline of farm income. We need an objective appraisal of the use of funds spent in this area, and we need to know how we can best aid 75,000 Rural Areas Development Committee members now working at this task.

4) A careful review of government research and education activities. Perhaps there is need for institutions in this field to shift their activities to a greater extent toward the promotion of adjustments within agriculture and toward the discovery of new uses and markets.

5) A study of government programs in wheat, dairy products, feed grains, vegetable oils, cotton, and other commodities. Also a study of the proper role of the Commodity Credit Corporation.

6) An intensive review of Public Law 480 — our

Food for Peace program — to determine how it can be extended and expanded without injuring commercial markets.

It if were established by our government, such a bipartisan blue-ribbon commission could teach us a great deal. It could help to rid us of some of our archaic policies and some of our misconceptions, and help plot a course for a future agricultural policy that would be affirmative rather than negative, designed to make use of our abundant production rather than to smother and cripple it.

V

The Quality of Life

We are the standard-bearers in the only really authentic revolution, the democratic revolution against tyrannies. Our strength is not to be measured by our military capacity alone, by our industry, or by our technology. We will be remembered, not for the power of our weapons, but for the power of our compassion, our dedication to human welfare.

That welfare demands that full scope be given to social as well as mechanical invention. The founders of this nation understood this and sought to secure conditions favorable to the "pursuit of happiness." They recognized man's spiritual nature, and the needs of emotion and intellect. They knew that only part of the pain and pleasure of life is to be found in material things.

Each person has capacities not possessed by any other. The free society alone can release these capacities. The fact is that we have released human creative talent to a much greater degree than ever before in history. The productive power of American industry is one proof of this. But we need to extend this creative power into the cultural and spiritual areas of life. And we need to prove that human brotherhood, under freedom, has more power to fire the imagination of peoples of the world than any purely materialistic system. Viewed in these terms, brotherhood has never before been so strong a requirement for our national security.

I see, in the America of tomorrow, the true spiritual and cultural capital of the world. It will be heir to man's loftiest hopes and achievements. It will be a land of many faces and religions, of peoples cosmopolitan and understanding of each other — yet each cherishing their unique traditions. It will be a land such as never existed before, and it will vibrate with the creativity and unleashed talents of millions.

The day will come. But to speed its arrival we must strive to improve and refine the American character, which is humane and good, but far from the ideal. Our social concepts — our human relations — have not caught up with our technical knowledge and practices. The technology that produces weapons of mass destruction has not really been applied to the true miracles possible: cleansing the earth of disease, educating mankind, bringing forth from the earth the food to feed and the fibre to clothe the poor of the world. To do so, we will have to internationalize our concepts of social welfare and social justice. We must seek for others throughout the world the same goals we seek for ourselves.

We live in an era of potential catastrophe; our physical sciences have made it so. We live in an era of potential glory; our minds and spirits together can make it so. The real strength of this America, this free society, is the quality of its heritage and its people — people with a commitment to freedom and social justice.

Education and Youth

There is one common denominator in all the challenges facing us, one word that keeps recurring — education. It is the key word when we talk about problems of employment, of expanding our economy, of improving ourselves and increasing our enjoyment of life, of revitalizing our institutions — or even of winning the Cold War. In a sense, the whole of this book is addressed to the needs and role of education. This chapter is concerned with education in its basic sense, where it matters most, where it begins — the education of our youth.

Education, we all agree, is a necessity for all. It must now become a reality for all. I think of education as a process that demands greater flexibility in training opportunities — the kind of flexibility that relates education to the needs of a rapidly changing society. Knowledge — brainpower — must become the chief national product of America, and education our chief national industry. How else can we successfully combat poverty and unemployment, and how can civil-rights legislation, however good, prove to be anything more than a hollow victory?

Two out of three of the unemployed today do not have a high-school education. It is obvious that we must keep our young people in school longer, but have we looked deeply enough to find the answers? Why are there so many dropouts? Are they leaving, in part, because what they are being taught is unrelated to the world they know outside the classroom?

It is essential that we guarantee the constitutional rights of every American. But what good are those rights without the guarantee that all Americans be provided an education that will enable them to participate fully and creatively inAmerican life? We may meet the challenge of school desegregation, but that isn't the whole story. We have a long way to go to overcome the tragic results of segregated education and the fact that we have, for so long, denied Negroes the opportunity for higher education.

Can we provide the kind of education that will reach out to the dropouts, the illiterates, the unskilled, the sharecropper children, the slum children, and the bewildered children, caught in the pressure-cooker atmosphere of the big city? I think we can — if we explore new ideas and new proposals, and if we are not afraid to try them, no matter how harsh the criticism from those content with methods used back in Dickens' day. This will require a heavier investment in education on the part of the Federal Government. It will require underwriting of more research and a stepping-up of activities as a clearing house for this research.

The Federal Government must also provide greater opportunities in higher education. The education bills we enacted in 1963 broke new ground for aid to colleges and the college student. But we are still remote from our goals.

Last spring, 400,000 high-school graduates who were in the upper half of their classes failed to go on to college. In some cases, there was inadequate guidance and lack of incentive, but the major reason was lack of money. The waste is tragic, the loss irretrievable.

College enrollments are increasing more than 8 per cent per year and are making staffs and physical plants inadequate. The cost of education keeps increasing, too, and higher education is growing more and more out of the reach of too many American youths. There is the danger of limiting college education to the children of the well-to-do and the college-educated, which could lead to a society divided along lines of cultural class. Ours is a country dedicated to equal opportunity for every citizen, regardless of race, creed, national origin, geography — or economic condition. We need all the talent we can get, but something more than just a national talent pool is at stake: Democracy itself is at stake.

Considering our over-all Federal budget, I am appalled at how little stress is placed on the importance of improving and training the mind as part of national security and defense. Surely our future demands that we provide increased government support for higher education, for the educational needs of American youth destined to live with the complex social, political, and technological problems of our tense world.

The question of whether the Federal Government should participate in educational support is a tired and specious one. It was fully answered over a hundred years ago by the passage of the Morrill Land Grant Act. The answer then was Yes, an affirmation that has been repeated time and again. That legislation provided the basis for the development of the land-grant colleges. Today, these sixty-eight colleges and universities enroll approximately one-fifth of all the college students in the United States, although they constitute only one-thirtieth of the institutions of higher learning.

The government relies on the universities to do those things which cannot be done by government personnel in government facilities. It turns to the universities for basic research in the field of agriculture. The remarkable competence of American agriculture is due in no small part to the research, experimentation, and extension work of the universities. The government turns to the universities in many other fields — defense, medicine, and public health, to name a few.

In all these ways, the government has a tremendous investment in education. And there has been a dollars-and-cents return of impressive proportions. A publication of the Chase Manhattan Bank recently summarized one economic study which indicated that 24 per cent of the increase in the gross national product from 1929 to 1957 — and 44 per cent of the increased production per worker — could be attributed to the higher level of education among the labor force. In addition, it reported, increased knowledge and its application accounted for another 17 per cent of the growth in the gross national product and 31 per cent of the rise in the output per employee. The publication concluded: "The record shows that the growth in the gross national product resulting from education has been sufficient to cover much of the cost of our school system despite the rapid rise in enrollment and expenditures. Thus, year for year, as well as over time, a large part of the expenditure on education is self-financed." This refers to the total expenditures for education at all levels. The Federal amounts spent are a minute part of total costs, less than 4 per cent.

National defense and security, national health, and national economic growth are direct reflections of the skills and resources developed by our schools. Nowhere have we gotten so much for so little cost. Here is the ultimate line of defense for our country.

And although the bogey is continually raised,

there has never been any evidence of Federal control in the long history of this Federal education partnership.

The agricultural and mechanical colleges which the Federal Government started supporting a hundred years ago had a specific purpose. How to implement this purpose, or interference with subject matter or teaching method, has never remotely been an issue. The Department of Agriculture has participated with the land-grant schools in experimental stations and extension programs. These have been free to initiate and carry out any research deemed necessary. The 10,000 county agents and home demonstrators in 3,000 counties in America are as free as the individuals they work with.

Federal participation in education does not imply control. On the other hand, how free is a scientist if he does not have equipment and facilities with which to do research? How free is a college to do a good job in language training if it cannot afford laboratories and modern equipment? How free is an able student to get into college if there is no dormitory there to house him, teacher to teach him, or classrooms in which to study?

The extraordinary demands on education in the decade ahead of us cannot be met by state-local-private sources alone. The Federal Government must provide more assistance to institutions of higher learning. To do so is an investment, not an expense — a stimulus to freedom and a protection to a diversified system of education, not a stultifying control.

As a former college teacher, I cannot leave the subject of higher education without offering some suggestions to my former colleagues and friends in the colleges and universities of America. I am proud of the vigor and the integrity of American higher education. I offer my criticisms because of this pride, and because I have always felt that the lines of communication between our scholars and our political officials should be kept open.

While colleges have a legitimate role as "islands of contemplation," there is a concurrent responsibility to develop more experienced and toughened young minds than are now being shaped in sheltered academic situations. The campus must open its gates wider to the currents of American and world political, economic, and social opinion. I should like to see the swirl and beat of controversy developing much more freely. I am dismayed when I hear a college official tell an audience that "we won't get into controversial subjects here." Disagreement and dissent are basic to democracy. Where but on a college campus can they be expressed more thoughtfully and to better purpose? Are they not part of the educational process? There is nothing more stimulating to young men and women coming to intellectual maturity than exposure to the realities of politics and public issues of all kinds — and exposure to unpopular, nonconformist, but challenging points of view.

There is a need for clearer understanding on the part of college graduates of the mainsprings of national power and the motivations of national conduct. Too often, a student can emerge from a series of courses in economics, history, and government without a real understanding of their interrelationship, without making the kind of synthesis that will prepare him to face, and help to solve, the problems of his society and his nation.

My teaching days gave me a lasting respect for the American educational system. They also gave me constant concern that it always seek ways and means for improvement. My government years have added another concern — that we utilize our educational system to feed more brainpower into the machinery of American foreign policy.

"By their works ye shall know them," and the works of peace are imperative in American foreign policy. Our vast food abundance has improved human life throughout the world in the Food for Peace program. American medical research and know-how have helped other nations in their struggle against disease — "health for peace." And there is still another major area to help us achieve our goal — "education for peace."

The one resource most of the needy countries have in abundance is manpower. But it is, for the most part, untrained and unskilled. Unfortunately, Russia accepted the challenge first. In Communist nations, new universities sprang up, new laboratories, large scholarship programs for talented students; in newly independent and needy countries, the Communists earned gratitude and even loyalty by providing technical and vocational training — sometimes, ironically, for the use of American equipment gathering rust.

We have not completely ignored the opportunity of "education for peace." The Fulbright program has been a great act of creative statesmanship, bringing our academic community into closer contact with the world of foreign scholarship. Through our atomic-energy program, foreign scientists have been trained in American research institutions. In economic development programs, foreign technicians have been brought here every year for training. The State Department has brought over leaders in many fields. Our great private foundations have given assistance to foreign educational institutions. And with the establishment of the Peace Corps, we have come closer to meeting the needs and the opportunities of "education for peace."

But there is still a major barrier to economic and social progress in underprivileged nations — a lack of trained public administrators and private managerial talent. It is one of the great tragedies in developing nations that there are so few nonmilitary citizens who have the necessary training for government service or private management. Be default, juntas come to power and stay in power, or are overthrown by other juntas.

We need to mobilize public administration and private management talents of this country to help develop the leadership potential as well as the technical resources of less-developed nations. We are in a position to help establish educational and training institutions abroad, adapted to local needs, to encourage greater educational exchange and to put education on an international level.

I have emphasized higher education in this country and the untrained, unskilled manpower of needy nations. It is a paradox that our land of wealth is also needy. Our economy is lagging far behind its potential in providing jobs for adults and young people. Our elementary and secondary school systems often fail to provide the education each American child rightfully deserves. Our society unfortunately considers vocational education to be second-rate education and has never provided adequately for such instruction. It still is not doing so — despite the fact that American society, urban and rural, is undergoing transformations that radically alter traditional modes of employment, family living, and social organization.

I began a sermon in 1958 that I am still preaching in 1964 — the need for a Youth Employment Opportunities Act. Such an act would save lives, natural resources — and money. Such an act, opponents have replied, is a classic example of a "do-gooder" experiment.

Six years is a long time to wait, but I am hopeful at the time of writing that this act will, in one form or another, soon become law. S.1, as it is currently called, is a revised version of the original bill, S.404, which was caught in the grip of the House Rules Committee, despite its unqualified endorsement by the Department of Labor and the White House. The act is even more vital today than when it was first proposed.

The Youth Employment Opportunities Act would provide assistance to thousands upon thousands of young people victimized by the problems of sluggish economic growth, inadequate educational systems, automation, urbanization, and social disorientation. It does not offer solutions to these basic problems — which we must work out in other ways — but it is a means for restoring these young people to productive and meaningful lives, and for alleviating the impact of unemployment on individuals and on society at large.

The act establishes a Youth Conservation Corps to take in school dropouts, youngsters who have failed to acquire a basic education, and those who have failed to locate permanent employment. These are the youth who should have the high hopes of their generation, but instead have become prisoners of their environment, prisoners of discouragement.

The Corps can break this chain of self-perpetuating defeats and failures, lift discouraged youth from depressing surroundings, and give them valuable skills. I see Youth Conservation Corps enrollees learning automotive repairing, baking, carpentry, conservation, electrical wiring, masonry, metalworking, photography, plumbing, sign painting, surveying and mapping, truck driving — any and all the skills needed to get and hold a job.

The Youth Conservation Corps is designed for young men sixteen through twenty-one years of age. Minimum enrollment is six months, maximum enrollment two years. Wages are $60 per month plus board, lodging, clothing, tools and equipment, medical care, and other necessities. Enrollees are to be selected by state employment agencies on the basis of population figures of the states, with special preference given to areas of substantial unemployment. Two-thirds of the Youth Conservation Corps would work on lands of the national forests, national parks, and other Federal conservation agencies; one-third would be available for work on state forests and parks on a 50-50 matching basis. Technical training and other educational skills would be provided after work periods through arrangements made by the Department of Health, Education, and Welfare and local educational authorities.

A local Area Youth Employment Program for unemployed men and women sixteen through twenty-one years of age was also provided for in S.1. Through the use of 50-50 matching grants, local public or private nonprofit agencies are to pay the wages of youngsters for useful full-time or part-time work not being performed by regular employees. The program will depend on local initiative for formulating local employment program proposals. In order to be approved, the local programs must increase the employability of the enrollees or enable them to resume or maintain school attendance. Testing, counseling, job-development, and job-referral services are to be provided for every enrollee.

The provisions of the Youth Employment Act differ from those of the National Service Corps — the so-called domestic peace corps. The National Service Corps is a vehicle through which public-spirited persons who already possess considerable training and skills can contribute their time and talent to others. It is also an opportunity for adding years of usefulness to older citizens' lives. The purpose of the Youth Employment Act is to establish programs that can begin to cope with the problem of unemployment among youth while also helping to conserve our national resources and to achieve general public needs.

We are alarmed by juvenile delinquency. We know that 800,000 young citizens are looking for full-time jobs, that almost 16 per cent of out-of-school teenagers are unemployed (and the rate continues to rise each month). We are just now beginning, under President Johnson's leadership, to understand the size of our problem.

I first introduced my youth bill in 1959. It was approved by the Senate, but the House failed to act. In 1962, the labor and public-welfare committees of both houses of Congress approved the measure, but the bill was stalled in the House Rules Committee. Last year, I introduced what was called the Youth Employment Act of 1963. A Gallup poll revealed that almost 89 per cent of the country approved the measure. The Senate passed the bill in 1963. Yet final action in the House was still pending in mid-1964.

These proposals, in one form or another, have been before Congress for nearly six years. There is nothing novel, unknown, or irresponsible about them. But while Congress has been considering them, the problem of unemployment among youth has become graver and now threatens to get out of hand.

I do not doubt that we shall solve this problem as we somehow seem to solve most of our problems — in time. But we are delayed considerably — while the casualties mount — by those who cry "do-gooder" or worry about the "welfare state." Earlier in this book, I tried to explain my concept of the welfare society. I believe it to be a twentieth-century version of the society conceived of by our founding fathers, propounded by the most thoughtful of philosophers, sanctioned by the compassionate spirit of all religious leaders.

"Do-gooders" all! I regret that there is so much cynicism attached to the term today, and that those who cry "do-gooder" mean it to be insulting. I certainly don't mind being called one. It puts me in the best company in the world.

Our Cultural Needs

The notion that government control inevitably follows government support limits and frustrates us in many areas besides education. Our cultural activities generally suffer because of this unjustified fear. We are the only major nation in the Western world whose government offers little or no direct financial assistance to the arts.

Great Britain, on whose institutions many of ours are modeled, long had a tradition of private patronage of the arts. But during World War II, when all resources were being taxed to the utmost in a struggle for survival, the British Government began to support such enterprises as music and the theater to provide solace and encouragement to embattled Britons. It realized that danger and hardship could be better endured by people who shared in the creative cultural expressions of mankind.

Since then, the theory that the Parliament should appropriate funds for the arts has won consistent approval from both Conservative and Labour governments. The Royal Opera and Ballet are thus supported. Orchestras, repertory theaters, museums, painters, sculptors, and composers enjoy the patronage of the British Government. The artistic talents of Britain are encouraged and developed in a manner befitting the precious resources they represent.

Has this stultified the talent of Britain? *New York Times* drama critic Howard Taubman had this to say: "There is a ferment in the British creative world. New young voices are raised in the theater, music, graphic arts. Sometimes they are angry and derisive; sometimes they probe quietly. They are sources of stimulation and provocation."

In France, the Opera, the Opera Comique, the Comedie Francaise are national instituions known throughout the world. France is proud of their contributions to the world of art and rightfully so.

West Berlin, only recently resurrected from the debris of World War II, has built a 1,900-seat opera house at a cost of $7 million in federal and city tax monies. Its performances are subsidized at the rate of $4 per seat per performance. The Berlin Philharmonic Orchestra receives federal and city subsidies of over $625,000. Indeed, the arts are major weapons in the competition for men's minds and are fully recognized and appreciated as such in this border city.

Throughout the Western world many great artistic achievements are today being brought about with the support of government. The Bayreuth Wagner festival, La Scala Opera of Milan, the Vienna State Opera, the Amsterdam Concertgebouw Orchestra are all government-supported, all flourishing.

Why is it that these governments can enourage the arts — arts that are enjoyed within each country and admired throughout the world — while ours cannot?

The arts have not been stifled or subjugated in these lands, and neither would they be in the United States. The contention that government support for the arts in our country would lead to their sterility or debasement is a counsel of fear. It is born of a strange lack of faith in the American people and their institutions — both governmental and artistic.

We do harm to ourselves by accepting the thesis that art and democratic government are natural enemies. Other nations and other freedom-loving peoples know that this is not so. And ironically, while many of our artists of great ability find it difficult to earn a living and many of our art institutions fail for lack of funds, governments with far less financial resources have come to the aid of American art. In recent years, the Italian Government has granted a subsidy to the Chicago

Lyric Opera Company, and the West German Government has pledged $2.5 million for the new Metropolitan Opera House in New York's Lincoln Center.

With several of my colleagues, I have introduced legislation calling for a national arts and cultural development act. It would go beyond the idea of the National Council on the Arts envisaged by President Kennedy. We do need the Council to serve as a national focal point, bringing together the most qualified and knowledgeable persons in the arts. We need the Council to allow these persons to bring their thinking to the attention of the government and the general public. But we need to do much more if we are to match the kind of policies that have so greatly stimulated artistic and cultural development in other nations of the West for so many years.

We need a National Arts Foundation to provide grants-in-aid to private groups and states in support of those projects which can make significant contributions to the arts. Earlier proposals for such a foundation have been limited to the "visual and performing arts." The need however, is to stimulate the arts generally. In addition to aiding artistic and cultural production, the legislation we have introduced would help support projects meant to encourage and assist artists living in the United States. It would help in training, in the commissioning of works, and in research, surveys, and planning in the arts. The bill would also make the activities of museums — including art-appreciation courses, public lectures, training classes — eligible to receive assistance.

All the activities assisted by the National Arts Foundation would be undertaken by private groups demonstrating the highest professional standards and with appropriate state agencies concerned with the arts. The Federal Government would not be directly involved in any of the endeavors that might receive support. In almost all cases, the grants to private groups would not exceed one-half of the total cost of any project or production.

In a system such as ours, the issue of government control in such an undertaking is really a nonexistent one. We have had some experience. Back in the 1930'd, the New Deal's Works Project Administration subsidized various types of theater. Not only did WPA projects train and develop some of the finest talents functioning in our theater today; some of the plays produced were harshly critical of policies of the government that was paying for them. Freedom, American-style, is a vigorous thing. We should have more faith in it.

Toward Greater Mental Health

The major theme of my address last year to the National Association of Mental Health was that the continued life of the world depends, fundamentally, on the mental health of the world's leaders. And, I added, the emotional instability of a single man, if left untended, could impose monstrous penalties on our society.

I remember the date of that speech well. The

very next day was November 22, 1963 — when the President of the United States was killed in an irrational, senseless act. And the man accused of perpetrating this act had been diagnosed, a decade earlier, as being in need of professional psychiatric care.

This was the most shocking example of the tragic toll taken by mental disorders in the United States. We have barely begun the great work of reducing the staggering backlog of unmet psychiatric needs in our communities — care of the sick young and sick old, of the institutionalized and the "walking wounded," of the juvenile delinquent and the criminal adult, of the alcoholic, and of the potential killer.

One of President Kennedy's most cherished projects was a massive new plan to deal with mental illness and retardation by Federal support of state agencies and by cooperative, united action in the government and on the part of voluntary groups. His administration proposed giving grants to states and to communities for the construction and manning of mental-health centers and the training of teachers. While the Senate approved an eight-year program to cost $847 million, the House-approved bill allowed for a three-year program amounting to only $238 million. The difference represented the cost of staffing the community mental-health centers, which was strongly opposed in the House.

A compromise bill was passed and signed into law by President Kennedy barely a month before he died. It provides $329 million for construction and projects covering the next three- and four-year periods, $150 million of this to be used for construction of community mental-health centers. The rest of the money is to be used for research centers, the training of teachers, and various grants for construction of facilities.

Although it fell short of his hopes, President Kennedy signed Public Law 88-164 with great enthusiasm. It was a momentous first step, representing one of the boldest programs in the field of mental health ever undertaken.

Now community health centers are being built which will substantially reduce the population of our large, centralized public mental institutions. They will provide preventive services, early diagnosis, and comprehensive treatment on both an in-patient and an out-patient basis. They will also provide all-important aftercare for discharged patients.

Unfortunately, the final version of the bill did not provide the necessary funds to staff these facilities. We must now go on to authorize them. This effort at economy was obviously shortsighted, for it tends to continue one of the most shocking, indefensible wastes in the world — the waste of human lives. (One reason given for not allocating funds for the cost of staffing the centers was that old bugaboo — the fear of Federal control.)

We need more psychiatrists, psychiatric social workers, and related personnel. There is a desperate need for greater cooperation among all levels of government — Federal, state, and local — in launching a major drive on mental illness and for the care and rehabilitation of the mentally retarded. In this area, as in all basic problem areas of American life, the role of private and voluntary groups is invaluable. Not only is the scientific knowledge of the doctor needed; the rehabilitation of the mentally ill and retarded also requires the understanding and professional competence of the social worker, the employment office, private industry, and government agencies.

Aside from the suffering and anguish caused by our failure to move ahead swiftly in this field, the actual dollar costs to our economy are enormous. I cannot understand the point of view that denies the modest investment now that would save hundreds of millions of dollars in annual tax monies later. For, unless we act soon, we will have to spend these monies for welfare purposes, for crime prevention and imprisonment, for the many incredibly high direct costs of mental illness in our society. And then there is the incalculable cost of a November 22, 1963.

Nevertheless, the step we have taken, with all its limitations, is a historic beginning. For one thing, it is a sign that we have learned, in this century, to deal with mental illness compassionately and intelligently. We no longer recoil before it, or panic in its presence. As a society, we have begun to handle it — to take steps to reduce, reverse, and cure it.

It is urgent that we do so. Sanity, logic, reason, emotional stability — all the goals of mental health — have intimate bearing on the life and death of our civilization. It is not individuals alone who can be afflicted with emotional instability and irrational behavior. Whole groups and entire nations can be swept into patterns of behavior that may have terrible consequences to themselves and to man's future.

We have seen it in our time. In the case of Nazi Germany, the results were devastating to the world. The primary victims of the Nazi madness were Jews; 6 million, more than one-third of all the Jews in the world, were killed by the Nazis or their accomplices. And considerably more than double that number of persons were killed on battlefields alone in World War II. The Soviet Union under Stalin also offered us evidences of madness gripping a nation's leaders. Now, in this thermonuclear age, we live in a world that could be quickly destroyed by mental instability. It is a world with no margin for error, in which the judgment or miscalculation of a powerful leader can bring the death of civilization.

Avoiding World War III is not just a social, economic, political, or military problem. It is a problem that requires the mobilization of every conceivable skill in human relations, including what we know about mental health. Sometimes nations are ruled by irrational men. But more often, the decisions and acts of nations are determined by a complicated psychological interplay among a nation's leaders, institutions of government, and people. It is important that we fully understand the mood and attitudes of both the leaders and the peoples of the nations with which we deal. To achieve this, we need to bring psychological and psychiatric judgment into the mainstream of our own evaluation and policy-making processes.

I think, too, that racial and religious prejudice is a disease, a mark of emotional disorder. The absurd generalizations of the bigot may be refuted or shattered time and again, and yet he will continue to mouth them, for he is neither a logical man nor a rational one.

We now have active in our country a small minority of the extreme, or radical, right. Its members are against civil rights, against the United Nations, against social security, against the flouridation of water, against disarmament, against, against, against — really against people, I suppose. They see evidence of sinister conspiracy behind all such causes. The civil-rights movement is an effort to "mongrelize" the race. The United Nations is out to take away the sovereignty of the United States. Flouridation of water is part of a plot to weaken us for the Communist "takeover." The last four presidents of the United States are supposed to have been in some way part of the Communist conspiracy — either duped by it or willing or unwilling accomplices of it.

Those who have this view of life suffer, I fear, from acute detachment from reality. Their fanaticism is as disturbing as the fanaticism of the extreme left was in the 1920's. Then it seemed that the Soviet Union could do no wrong, the United States could do no right. The extreme left fervently believed in the extravagant promises of Marxism. Even when all the evidence showed that the dream turned into a nightmare, its devotees persisted in their unreal belief.

It is no coincidence that some of the leaders of the extreme left of three decades ago have since turned up as leaders of the extreme right. They still see the world in total black or white; they are still looking for immediate and final answers in a complex world which rarely, if ever, offers immediate and final answers. They still substitute dogma for creative thought; they are still angry, afraid — and disturbed.

We are wrong when we react emotionally to such emotionalism. We are wrong when we let the extremist in our midst frighten or goad us into impulsive acts of repression. No witch-hunt ever served its stated purpose. All have done considerable damage along the way to our freedoms and our self-respect.

"The best revenge on your enemy is not to be like him." The best way to handle the fanatic or extremist is to avoid his tactics and to keep the faith in democracy that he lacks. We have real problems in abundance; it is tragic when the fantasies of the extremist occupy so much of our time.

I do not wish to seem casual about the threat of the extremist in the United States. But I do think that we have achieved a certain level of mental health in this nation — a stability and toughness — that will prevent the fanatic from ever sounding more than a single strident note in the otherwise harmoniously orchestrated American theme.

On Welcoming New Americans

Oscar Handlin wrote in the introduction to his Pulitzer Prize-winning book, *The Uprooted*: "Once I thought to write a history of immigrants in America. Then I discovered the immigrants *were* American history."

No one can seriously question the role that immigrants have played in shaping the United States and making it great. Yet, since 1924, the laws of this nation have barred immigration to the United States upon grounds that have no basis in logic, in fact, or in morality. The "national origins" quota system seeks to maintain some mythical racial and ethnic purity by apportioning immigration visas among the nations of the world in proportion to the ethnic composition of our 1920 population. The system is not only discriminatory; it violates a prime national interest — the fullest use of our potential human resources.

From the days of Plymouth Rock and Jamestown until the early decades of this century, this country was open to immigrants of all nations who met reasonable standards of health and character. Our country became stronger and more creative as each new wave of immigration reached our shores and contributed its own particular energies and traditions. I am proud that this is not a country of monolithic conformity, but rather a country with a vital and vibrant admixture of many peoples, tongues, and talents. These differences, I believe, have contributed to our peculiar genius for invention, for experimentation, for progress, and for world leadership.

The National Origins Act of 1924 and its most recent successor, the Immigration and Nationality Act of 1952, renounced the American open-door policy toward free immigration. The first thing these laws did was to limit the total number of annual immigrants. I have no quarrel with that basic policy. There must be a limit to any country's capacity to absorb new citizens. While I might disagree as to how high that limit should be, I do not advocate totally unrestricted immigration.

Today our immigration law authorizes the admission of approximately 156,000 quota immigrants annually from outside the Western Hemisphere. The figure is fixed at a sixth of 1 per cent of our 1920 population — that is, less than a tenth of 1 per cent of our present population.

But our laws go further. They split up these 156,000 people among the various countries of the world in proportion to the number of Americans living in 1920 who could trace their origin to a given country. As a result, by far the larges quota, 65,000, goes to Great Britain, at the expense of practically all the other countries.

The countries of southern and eastern Europe are particularly hard hit. Consequently, the quotas of such countries as Italy and Greece have become heavily oversubscribed, while Great Britain does not even use half its allotment. Since, under our laws, all unused numbers are declared forfeited, fewer than 100,000 immigration permits are actually used, with 50,000 to 60,000 going begging each year.

The inherent discrimination against southern and south-eatern Europeans is only part of the unhappy tale. Singled out for special discrimination are the inhabitants of the so-called Asia-Pacific triangle. Here — in India, Pakistan, China, Japan, and neighboring countries — live half of the earth's population. Under our immigration laws, we admit not more than 100 persons per year from each of these nations. Such discrimination is patently wrong.

I shall not go into the demeaning business of seeking to "prove" how much Italians or Hungarians or Greeks have contributed to the United States. Their acts speak for themselves. And each man should be judged as an individual, not by his place of birth.

The present law is predicated upon the theory of a racial or cultural elite. There is no such elite in those terms. There should be no privilege of race or national origin — no privilege except the privilege of ability. We will be a better nation as soon as we get rid of the nonsensical notion that one kind of blood or skin color is better than another kind of blood or skin color. This notion has sometimes driven us to an unhappy position in world affairs.

There are two good bills now in Senate subcommittee — S.747 and S.1932 — which would remove this skeleton from our national closet. S.747 was introduced by Senator Philip Hart, and I am among its thirty-three co-sponsors. S.1932 is the administration measure, based on recommendations made to Congress by the late President Kennedy. There are differences in detail in the two bills, but both would eliminate the worst inequities and deceptions of the present law.

Senator Hart has explained what his bill seeks to do:

1) For the present national-origins system, it substitutes a formula based on equality and fair play for all nations. The bill beings by increasing the total number of quota visas that can be issued annually from about 156,000 to 250,000. Of this enlarged total, the bill distributes 80,000 visas among the countries of the world outside the Western Hemisphere in the same proportion that the size of their population bears to the world population. Another 120,000 visas are distributed among the different countries on the basis of their recent postwar experience. Both these ways of calculating quota visas eschew the outdated census of 1920 as a criterion for determining America's immigration needs.

Finally, it eliminates the Asia-Pacific triangle clauses of the old law, which have no legitimate place in our public policy. Persons with as much as one-half Asian ancestry would now come in under the quota of their country of birth or citizenship, like other immigrants.

2) The bill provides for the yearly admission of a reasonable number of refugees from all over the world. The steady trickle of escapees from Eastern Europe, the flight of Chinese into Hong Kong, and the Jewish exodus from North Africa and parts of South America — all point out the need for some permanent arrangement (though obviously, the

solution to today's refugee problems does not lie in mass migration to the United States). At present, all the refugees, such as the Hungarian "parolees," have come in under special laws, and they need a special law to stay. The reform bill reserves one-fifth (50,000) of the total number of annual quota visas to refugees.

3) By going outside the national quotas to admit persons who possess skills and talents urgently needed, S.747 eliminates the periodic need for special legislation in this area. A recent National Science Foundation report said that there was both room and need for foreign-born scientists and engineers.

Our current immigration laws are a particular affront at this point in our history, when we are seeking to extend human rights here and abroad. The immigration policy of the 1960's will go a long way toward determining the kind of country America will be a hundred years from now. It must be based on the same democratic principles that made our present greatness.

The enactment of a sound bill now will help restore the image of the United States as a progressive, humane member of the international community. And it will enrich our national life through the infusion of new vitality, new cultures, and new ideas.

There is one characteristic of the immigrant — the new American — that is often overlooked. He brings with him, often enough, a nostalgia and longing for the place he left behind. But he brings with him something else — a fierce and beautiful loyalty to the United States. You can understand this best if you personally know new Americans and their children, whether they are Minnesota farmers or New York City textile workers.

Although these new Americans have found that our streets are not paved with gold, many of them have realized here the opportunity for the better life once denied them. And how they respond — with passion and devotion, with a love of our traditions and folk heroes that is often more fervently felt by them than by older Americans who take our freedoms for granted.

VI

The World About Us

The realization that what happens in the Middle East is as important to Americans as what happens in the Midwest was a long time in coming. Two World Wars and the incredible speeds of our time have shattered our isolationism forever. International affairs has become an important topic of conversation — and a matter of constant concern — to growing millions of Americans.

As a people, we have responded maturely to the role thrust upon us after World War II. Other nations have assumed roles of world leadership with arrogance, disdain, and dreams of further conquest and glory. We have shown deference to small nations in our dealings with them, and we have been responsive to their sensitivities and folkways to an unprecedented degree. Older powers, hardened to international leadership, have sneered at us for naivete or "do-goodism." We have acted not like an imperial power, but more like a senior partner (and sometimes like a junior one). This is the first time in world history that a nation has used its energies and resources outwardly, for the sharing of freedom and the good life, and not wholly inwardly for self-protection and self-satisfaction.

We have our flaws and our prejudices and our xenophobia. We have used such terms as "gooks" and "greasers." But on reflection, we have always become uneasy about using them; our instincts tell us that they are wrong. We are a people who have dreamed up such things as "CARE packages" and a "sister city" project (in which the people of an American city get to know and cooperate with the people of a city abroad). We join in "people-to-people" programs. We endow hospitals and orphanages throughout the world, even though our own are not always exemplary. As individuals and in groups, we give gifts of food and love. In our abundance, we have proven ourselves to be the most philanthropic people in the world — and have been somewhat less patronizing about it than might have been expected.

"Our age will be well remembered," Arnold Toynbee said recently, "not for its horrifying crimes nor its astonishing inventions, but because it is the first generation since the dawn of history in which mankind dared to believe it practical to make the benefits of civilization available to the whole human race."

I appreciate the historian's view of foreign-aid programs generally. His perspective is gratifying. Our times may not be remembered as the atomic or space age, but as the age in which one-third of the human race banded together to help the other two-thirds.

My own view has always been that the purpose of foreign aid is not just to fight a Cold War, but to build a better world. Our aid programs express the true voice of America, the spirit of our continuing revolution. We have only to look at the terse statistics of human need: 83 per cent of the world's people underfed, more than 60 per cent illiterate, 70 per cent sick or poorly housed. The ancient adversaries of mankind — poverty, hunger, disease, and ignorance — are the allies of tyranny; they are the real enemies of mankind, more than the militancy of a Mao or a Khrushchev. They grip large portions of the world. But today, the great zone of misery and despair that encircles the earth, including Latin America, Africa, the Middle East, and Asia, is being transformed by the knowledge that there is a better life within reach.

There are misconceptions about foreign

assistance, and it provokes harsh criticism. A Gallup poll recently reported that many Americans think it costs us far more than the $4 billion it does, or that it costs at least double the 5 per cent of our national budget it actually does.

One U.S. Senator has said: "If I believed the expenditure of this amount of money would stop the spread of Communism, I would support it. But in the light of history, how can anyone say it will stop Communism?" And another: "Foreign aid is the road to bankruptcy, and not a very long road at that."

These two statements were not made in 1963 or 1964. They come from the record of the stormy Senate debate on the Marshall Plan in 1948. We all know now that the Marhsall Plan was a key weapon in the defense of Europe against Communism. And rather than bankrupting the United States, the Marshall Plan created vast new markets for American business and enabled Europe to join the United States in helping the less-developed countries.

(The Marshall Plan had its legion of critics. So do many other proposals that appear inherently wise, moral, and in our self-interest. I sometimes wonder how the American Constitution was ever adopted. It passed the New York Convention by only one vote and was ratified by a bare margin in Virginia. How could so many virtuous and intelligent men have been so wrong in 1788 — and in 1948?)

The Marshall Plan, which built up the war-ravaged economies of Europe, was the first great success in our foreign-assistance program. The second success was the Point Four program, which sent trained technicians to various parts of the world. As a mark of its success, to this day Point Four is often thought of as the generic term for all American assistance. A third success is the Food for Peace program, which shares America's agricultural miracle with many peoples of the world. Since 1955, Food for Peace exports have amounted to more than $12.5 billion. Feeding the hungry is sufficient reason for this program. Yet it also provides us with substantial economic and national-security benefits. It strengthens our foreign policy and offers a graphic demonstration of the efficiency of the family-owned farm under a free-enterprise system. Today, U.S. food is reaching an average of 92 million people a day in more than 100 countries of the world.

A fourth success is the Peace Corps, one of the finest expressions of the American humane spirit. When President Kennedy first established the Peace Corps, he warned: "It will not be easy. None of the men and women [serving abroad] will be paid a salary. They will live at the same level as the citizens of the country which they are sent to, doing the same work, eating the same food, speaking the same language . . . I am hopeful that this will be a source of satisfaction to Americans and a contribution to world peace."

The hardships did not deter Americans, and how well the Peace Corps has worked out. Its success has given me particular satisfaction for, as President Kennedy pointed out in his 1961 message to Congress on its formation, I had sought the adoption of legislation calling for the Peace Corps concept the year before.

These are just four examples of our foreign-aid efforts, all meant to benefit people generally, not just an elite. Few undertakings in history have posed a greater challenge. The wonder is that we have made so much progress in so brief a time. The Magna Charta was signed over 700 years ago, and we are still struggling with basic questions of democratic government. Yet scarcely more than a decade since the historic launching of foreign aid, there is impatience with its progress.

We have reviewed and improved the program substantially in recent years, particularly through the Act for International Development of 1961, which established the over-all Agency for International Development. Of all current programs, the Alliance for Progress is of particular interest to me, for it is concerned with one of the most critical areas of the world. This is the cooperative endeavor by nineteen Latin American countries and the United States to share more fully in the spiritual and material riches available in the twentieth century. It is not merely a U.S. aid program; the Latin American countries are themselves charged with the major effort, and ours is the supplemental one. However, the dedication to the principles of demoncratic government must come equally from the United States as well as from them.

The Alliance for Progress is a bold challenge to those who cry, with Communists and other extremists, that mankind cannot be freed from its bonds of ignorance and poverty without the violent destruction of the existing system and the imposition of a dictatorship.

It is a cooperative venture undertaken in the belief that the processes of constitutional democracy can move sufficiently swiftly and decisively to accomplish vital, urgent social and economic changes. I am committed to the proposition, and this nation is committed to the proposition, that change — radical, revolutionary change — can come through orderly, peaceful processes.

We must understand that there would be trouble, violence, and disorder in Latin America even if there were no Communists and Castroites. Castro's Communism is the effect rather than the cause of the deep discontent that has prevailed over vast areas of Latin America. As one observer has put it, most Latin Americans were born on dead-end streets and feel that they are doomed to live there until the day they die. Lives of grinding poverty and voiceless desperation are commonplace; I have seen this for myself. Latin America is dynamite, and there have already been explosions right on our doorstep. Castro and his Communists are exploiting the tensions and the troubles of a corrupt and dying order. The destruction of Castro and his regime in Cuba will not in itself cure Latin America's ills, for Latin America is very sick. And it has been sick for many, many years — sick because of its own failures, sick in part because of our neglect.

I can cite a few figures that underscore the depth

of its problems. Latin America, where more than 200 million people live in an area 2.5 times as large as the United States of America, received less than 3 per cent of the total economic aid given by the United States from 1945 to 1960. Compare this with Europe, which received 41 per cent of our aid; with the Far East, which received 17.5 per cent; with the Near East, which received almost 12 per cent. A mere 2 per cent of all the people in Latin American countries own more than 50 per cent of the total wealth. Two-thirds to three-fourths of the Latin Americans live in unbelievable, abject poverty. Furthermore, there is really an explosion in the Latin American population. It doubled from 1920 to 1956, and is now increasing at an over-all rate of more than 2.5 per cent a year; in some of the Central American republics I recently visited, the rate runs as high as 3.5-4 per cent. The life span is being extended, yet, paradoxically, life expectancy throughout South and Central America is still less than forty-five years, while here in the United States it is seventy.

The problems illustrated by these statistics are in no way superficial. They are deep and enduring, embedded in the centuries-old hard crust of tradition and privilege. They demand a coordinated attack by the most daring and ingenious men of our times, with a commitment of human and material resources far beyond anything that we have contemplated thus far. The commitment of resources we have already made can only be judged as a beginning. I fear that unless we do far more we will lose all that has been done up to now.

Such a commitment should not be undertaken by the United States alone. We need to be reminded again and again that the Alliance for Progress is an alliance. It is a partnership. We are only a part of it, and if this alliance is to succeed, we — all of us in this hemisphere — must mobilize and commit the resources of all the nations of this hemisphere on a heroic scale. We can well ask our prosperous friends and allies of Western Europe to make their contributions, too, for the battle for freedom is a world-wide one.

But it is we who have joined the fight. After my first observation of the Alliance for Progress in action in Latin America, I returned to this country in a critical frame of mind. Now, after further visits and study, I am genuinely hopeful. Life magazine, in a recent editorial on the Alliance called "The Latin Sky Is Brighter," said that its goals "are nothing less than to raise the incomes, diversifty and integrate the economies, reform the tax and land structures, improve the health, housing, and schooling, and enlarge the freedom of 200 million people in the next eight years. Unlike the Marshall Plan, which rebuilt a damaged but going concern, the Alliance aims to shape a society and an economy that have not existed before." Not the work of a day or, most likely, a decade either. But a real beginning has been made.

Americans can be proud of the successes our help has produced. In India, which is receiving more assistance from the United States and other nations of the free world than any other of the less-developed countries, the rate of industrial production increased from 6.4 to 8 per cent in the year ending in March, 1963. Indian production of aluminum, for example, increased from 20,000 tons to 43,000 tons during that year. Its output of machine tools, essential for industrial development, expanded by more than 50 per cent.

They have not been written yet, but some day there will be a shelf full of books on technical-assistance achievements made possible by U.S. aid, and on the advances made in public and business administration and taxation. There are countless examples in the field of cooperatives (a special interest of mine), in the development of private enterprise through the extension of credit, and in the development of agriculture through a combination of technical assistance and agricultural credit.

A dramatic achievement of our assistance can be seen in the story of malaria eradication. In recent years, the number of malaria cases in the world has been cut from 350 million to fewer than 100 million. In some areas, the disease has been eliminated altogether. Better health pays other dividends, too; in some parts of India, the return on money invested in controlling malaria has been about fifty to one in increased industrial production, resulting in an increase in the Indian gross national product of some $500 million a year. In one rich region in northern India, the elimination of malaria increased the area of cultivated land by more than 400 per cent and the production of food grains by 130 per cent.

There are good signs of over-all economic

success. A recent analysis of 41 countries that have received over $300 million each in American assistance since the beginning of the program (or, where the population is less than 10 million people, have received at least $30 per person) shows that 33 have achieved substantial economic growth of at least 1.5 per cent per capita in increased income during each of the last five years. Fourteen of these countries have achieved complete self-sufficiency; another 11 have reached the point of adequate self-sufficiency, and less than 20 per cent of their total investment is now covered by foreign aid. In all the countries that have achieved both substantial economic growth and adequate self-sufficiency, there has also been a strengthening of democratic political institutions.

Another over-all measure of the success of foreign aid is the increase in trade with countries receiving our assistance. U.S. exports to Marshall Plan countries more than doubled from 1953 to 1962. Our exports to Japan more than tripled since 1950. In 32 countries receiving 80 per cent of the U.S. aid between 1957 and 1962, imports from the U.S. increased four times as fast as our economic aid did.

My belief is that the primary aim of foreign aid should be to build a more stable and interdependent world. Promoting trade serves this purpose — and at the same time a good deal of American self-interest. The less-developed countries are potentially vast markets for American goods and services. Foreign aid has had an increasingly beneficial effect on the American economy. Eighty per cent of all procurement now consist of American goods and services, and much of the remaining 20 per cent eventually comes back home. Almost every state in the Union is now beginning to experience the benefits of aid contracts.

Aid-financed U.S. procurement also gives U.S. business the opportunity to gain experience in world trade. Through foreign aid, American businessmen are learning the skills necessary to sell through regular commercial channels in years to come. As trade replaces aid, these skills, techniques, and contacts are sure to help them flourish in the world market.

Other nations understand this clearly. Some of the largest investments in the less-developed world are being made by the Federal Republic of Germany, in some of the (apparently) most unsettled countries, such as the Congo, Korea, and Brazil. The French Government, which spends considerably more than we do per capita for foreign aid, is expanding its program. The British, too, are increasing their foreign-aid program.

There have been many honest and valid criticisms of our aid program. There have also been major efforts to improve its organization and administration in the last few years. The new directions established by Congress in 1961 and implemented through AID include emphasis on long-term development projects, increased efforts to boost the contributions of other donor nations, emphasis on self-help and reform, and greater concentration and selectivity. Now 80 per cent of all our economic assistance is going to twenty countries, and 80 per cent of all military assistance to just ten countries.

The lack of a comprehensive approach to the problems of a country, and the lack of planning by the countries being aided, had been a major weakness of the program. Most aid had been given on a project-by-project basis, with little analysis of a country's basic needs. The present procedure is far better: Careful studies are made of each country, and comprehensive plans are set forth to make our assistance most effective. Except where urgent political considerations are involved, aid is given according to development priorities established for each country. Then studies are made of the country's progress and the degree of its self-help.

We now also encourage nations to study their problems and to formulate their own development plans. In the case of the Alliance for Progress, each Latin American country is required to submit development plans to an expert committee of the Organization of American States for review and recommendations.

Agreement on conditions before aid is granted has given us great selectivity. For many years, we assumed that such conditions constituted "strings," and interference in the domestic affairs of other countries and therefore, were wrong. It is now recognized that agreement on conditions in advance is a prerequisite for effective aid.

(Many of the changes were long overdue, and, obviously, there are others to be made. But I believe that foreign assistance has substantial support among Americans — despite occasional editorial outbursts against it. Support for foreign aid is strong, and growing stronger, among a most important group in American life — American businessmen. A recent study of 1,500 prominent businessmen by the Research Institute of America disclosed that the great majority of these business leaders consider foreign aid essential for promoting a self-supporting and prosperous community of free nations. These findings were hailed as "revolutionary in their significance" — and they are. They signify the end of economic and political isolation in the American business community and the existence of a new consensus concerning the responsibilities of the United States as the leader of the free world.)

Along with many others, I, too, believe there is still need for improvement in the aid program. We must make sharper distinctions among the areas of the world and our own potential for giving truly valuable assistance. The top priority should be given to Latin America. The Alliance for Progress should not be for us, as it is now, one of four regional programs in the same agency. It is different and, at the U.S. end alone, entails a wide variety of capital-development loans, economic loans, social-development loans and grants, and technical assistance. In our governmental structure, the Alliance program should be more independent than it is now, perhaps even an autonomous agency (like the Peace Corps).

A large U.S. lending program will probably continue to be necessary under the Alliance.

However, more of the capital-development lending should be shifted to the Inter-American Development Bank and other international finance institutions.

In various other areas of the world, such a many-sided program is unnessary for us. In the Far East, our military-oriented program must be maintained as long as needed to preserve nations from Communist aggression, while our programs of socioeconomic development must be increased. In the Middle East and such parts of Asia as India and Pakistan, multilateral agencies should supply much of the capital needed for large-scale development. Increasing the role of the World Bank and the International Development Association in promoting capital to countries like India, Pakistan, Iran, and Turkey can provide the capital assistance needed. It can also enlist greater economic participation on the part of our European allies.

In Africa, we should encourage Europeans to play the leading role in providing economic assistance. Meanwhile, we should continue our technical assistance, the Peace Corps, the Food for Peace program, limited economic aid, and other forms of assistance. The limited capital available to Africa should be channeled, in part, through multilateral agencies, where it will be matched by European funds.

Generally, we ought to encourage mulilateral, multinational, and international banking structures to do more of the financing. We can ask for proper representation on the boards of these banks and ask that Americans be included in substantial numbers in the secretariat or adminstration structures. The direct bilateral arrangement in financing involves us in each country's troubles. It is also very costly. By putting our emphasis on the multi-national organization, we will be able to get the help of others in financing world development. A multilateral agency also makes it easier to insist that certain conditions be met by recipients who may resent stipulations coming from Americans alone.

I think, too, that more of the foreign-aid program should be carried out on a contract basis by U.S. public and private groups and organizations and on a reimbursable basis by other government agencies. I do not mean, for one second, to reduce the Agency for International Development to the status of a contracting office; the foreign-aid program has to be operated under the direction of the Secretary of State and under the direct administration of AID. But AID itself should function less as a line agency, and more as a staff one, if its program is to become a more effective expression of American ideals and a better vehicle for applying our skills and knowledge elsewhere.

This is how foreign assistance gains its greatest meaning. Of all countries, Israel, small and young, has shown the way. In the past five or six years, it has extended technical assistance to almost eighty nations in Africa and Asia. Now it is sending technicians to Brazil, Ecuador, Bolivia, and Venezuela. Its most recent program is to train 200 Latin American students in modern agricultural methods. Israel is demonstrating that trained manpower is as essential in foreign aid as the big development loans that are being given by larger countries and international lending institutions. Israel is showing the value of extending its human resources to help.

For it is not enough to develop merely the economic and natural resources of a nation. We also must seek to train its people in the skills they need to achieve their potential. It is not enough to build a steel mill in a distant place without helping to train its people to operate its machinery. It is not enough to build a school; we must train local teachers so that they can help overcome ignorance and illiteracy. It is not enough to help finance the purchase of tractors and plows in backward rural areas; we must help train local farmers in effective techniques and the skills of modern farming. It is not enough to send supplies of medicines and hospital equipment; we must also train doctors, nurses, and hygienists.

Our record of foreign aid is unprecedented and daring. It is our way of showing true concern for the needs and aspirations of the restless millions of the world. Yet we run the risk of becoming known as a nation of bankers.

Dollars are not enough; they are spent and gone. Supplies are used up, equipment becomes obsolete. But education, knowledge, and the skills possessed by human beings are enduring.

We are a nation of doers, of builders and farmers and businessmen and scientists. We have the people with the skills. They — Americans by the thousands — must travel the globe, showing others how to use those skills. In this century, let us become known, above all, as a nation of teachers.

In Search of Disarmament

For some years, the clock on the cover of the *Bulletin of the Atomic Scientists* stood at three minutes to midnight — representing how close civilization was to the doom of a nuclear holocaust. The hands were moved back a few minutes in 1960, and then last year, when the limited nuclear-test-ban treaty was signed by the United States, Great Britain, and the Soviet Union, the hands of that clock were set back to twelve minutes to midnight, where they stand today. The symbolism is clear: Man has given himself a reprieve from destruction.

It was that close for a while — and it may be again. For the moment, it appears that man's instinct for survival is stronger than his suicidal urge. We have lived in the shadow of the bomb for almost two decades, and it has taken the combined resources and courage of thousands — scientists, statemen, soldiers — to avoid the fatal detonation. Still, nuclear weapons remain the greatest single threat to man's survival.

My own involvement in the quest for disarmament — particularly nuclear disarmament — dates back to 1949, my first year in the Senate. Three weeks after President Truman's announcement that he had ordered construction of a hydrogen bomb, I prepared an address for the

National Cathedral in Washington on the subject of "God, Man, and the Hydrogen Bomb." My comments were directed toward idealistic and long-range goals. I urged "universal disarmament" and an "unequivocal agreement to abolish war." But I knew then that we could never embark on a course of unilateral disarmament, that we needed a "control system" for any agreement, and that it was "our national interest, not just peace, that impelled us to make new efforts to negotiate."

Through the years, as Chairman of the Senate Disarmament Subcommittee, I worked with many persons seeking to find out what was most needed in the field of disarmament. We gradually became more knowledgeable and specific about what could be done. In October, 1956, the Subcommittee released a report on technical aspects of nuclear testing. In its introduction, I supported Adlai Stevenson's position calling for an effort to reach an agreement banning nuclear-weapons tests. We were clearly before our time.

During that year, I also began a series of letters to Secretary of State John Foster Dulles urging that more be done to work toward a test ban. The Subcommittee also sought to get Congress interested in the problem of nuclear fallout. We encouraged development of an efficient detection system and other matters basic to a test ban. We urged that more of the State Department staff work on test-ban and other disarmament projects. (It took four years of persuasion to get Congress to appropriate money, in 1960, to the State Department for this purpose.)

Throughout 1958, I kept up a steady stream of hearings, speeches, floor statements, and letters to the administration about a test ban. In the week before Easter, 1958, I spoke on the subject in the Senate every day, once for four hours. Lyndon Johnson, then majority leader, agreed to help, and urged all Democratic Senators to be in the chamber for this speech. (My key point was that the government should establish a basic new policy to separate the issue of the test ban from other disarmament issues.) The public response was overwhelming — greater than on any other statement I had made in the Senate. Americans appeared to be somewhat ahead of their elected officials in understanding the urgency of the test-ban proposal.

The hearings of the Subcommittee were directed more specifically to the subject of the test ban, stressing the need for more government research into the technical, scientific, and political issues involved — especially detection, identification, and inspection. But, by 1959, Congressional interest had waned because of the failure of negotiations with the Soviet Union. And, while President Eisenhower's interest in a test ban was undoubtedly genuine, he had little or no support from his own administration leaders.

In February, 1960, I introduced legislation to establish a National Peace Agency to expand and coordinate the government's efforts in disarmament. The bill did not get to the floor for action, but the following year, when I again introduced legislation — this time to establish an

Arms Control and Disarmament Agency — I had the support of the Kennedy Administration. Despite the Berlin crisis in the summer of 1961 (and near-universal skepticism about a test ban), the bill was approved and the Agency established in the fall of that year. The Agency quickly began detailed work on the technical and political problems of a test ban and other disarmament issues.

By the summer of 1962, it appeared that the United States had developed all the detection devices necessary to monitor tests "in the atmosphere, underwater, and in outer space." President Kennedy suggested to the Soviet Union that we start negotiations on this "limited" test-ban idea at that time. But the Soviet Union then rejected the idea.

When I returned from the Geneva test-ban negotiations in February, 1963, I reported that "unless some agreement can be reached within six months, the prospects of any test-ban agreement for many years would be nil." I privately renewed the suggestion for another United States offer to negotiate for the limited ban. When I learned of Senator Thomas Dodd's interest in the same idea, I joined with him in a resolution calling for a U.S. offer to negotiate on that basis. The resolution was introduced on May 2, 1963, and we were joined by thirty-two other Senators as co-sponsors — a fact that strengthened President Kennedy's hand when he encouraged the renewal of American-Soviet negotiations in his speech at American University, early in June.

The negotiations were successful. A draft treaty was initiated by the United States, Great Britain, and the Soviet Union on July 25. By the time the Senate ratified the treaty, on September 24, ninety-nine other nations had already subscribed to it.

The treaty banned tests in the atmosphere, in outer space, and underwater. It also provided for a continuance of negotiations on underground tests. Mankind had its breathing spell. The clock had moved back, away from midnight.

It had taken much effort, planning, and hope. I think that the limited test-ban treaty will stand as one of President Kennedy's greatest achievements. President Kennedy's address at the American University, which emphasized the mutual vulnerability of Russian and American peoples in the nuclear age, was a brave appeal to the minds of men, an appeal to an end to cant, prejudice, and unreasoning fear.

However, it was not alone his appeal to the American people that made the treaty a reality. It was also his administration's policy of dramatically strengthening our defenses while keeping open channels of communication with the Soviet Union. Actually, to bring about acceptance of a treaty the Soviet Union had, in the past, repeatedly rejected several major developments:

1) The Russians had seen our military strength rise dramatically since 1960, including the doubling of power in key areas in our strategic alert forces.

2) Russian leadership was shaken by President Kennedy's firmness in the crisis of October, 1962, when Soviet missiles were forced out of Cuba.

3) Soviet planners, in view of their internal problems, had strong reason to shift major resources from nuclear development to agricultural mechanization.

4) The Russians were deeply troubled by the growing political and military threats of Communist China, which appears to be bent on developing its own nuclear capability.

5) Finally, Russian leadership shares the American concern over the spread of nuclear weapons and the consequent increase in the danger of nuclear war.

The test-ban treaty is important in itself. But its greatest significance rests in the fact that Soviet leadership, for the first time, has given a clear signal that it understands the depth and massive extent of U.S. power — and is willing to come to terms with it.

The problem of arms control and reduction remains extraordinarily complex. A new round of disarmament talks opened in January, 1964, in Geneva with a seventeen-nation conference. Our hope should be sustained by these negotiations, no matter how frustrating or deadlocked they often appear to be. We have come to them with a strong position, but an open and reasonable attitude. Among the things we seek are means to prohibit the use (or the threat) of force to change boundaries or to interfere with access to territory or to extend control over territory by displacing established authorities.

We are also looking for a way to halt further increases in strategic armaments. Such an agreement would prevent the further expansion of the arms race — and could open the path to the reduction in all types of forces.

A third point — all of these, incidentally, have been enunciated by President Johnson — is our hope for a verified agreement to halt all production of fissionable materials for weapons use. Pending agreement on this, the United States is willing to achieve prompt reductions by having both sides close comparable facilities on a plant-by-plant basis, with mutual inspection.

We are also seeking to reduce the danger of war by accident, miscalculation, or surprise attack. As a move in this direction, in consultation with our allies, we are willing to discuss proposals for creating a system of observation posts. Another effort is to stop the spread of nuclear weapons to nations that do not now have them. This would call for agreement not to transfer nuclear weapons to the control of such nations; it would also stipulate that all transfers of nuclear material for peaceful purposes take place under effective national safeguards. In their peaceful nuclear activities, the major powers would also be called upon to accept the inspection they recommend for other states.

President Johnson took a first step toward reducing the production of atomic-weapons material in his State of the Union Message, in

January, 1964. He announced then that the Administration would close down four reactors producing plutonium and reduce, by 25 per cent, the production of enriched uranium by gaseous diffusion. There have since been further reductions, made possible by a combination of considerations. From the diplomatic point of view, we are emphasizing our willingness to slow the atomic arms race and to set an example for the Soviet Union. In no sense does this amount to unilateral disarmament; from the military standpoint, we can afford the reductions without impairing the nation's nuclear strength, since, in recent years, the production of weapons material has begun to exceed the actual requirements of weapons fabrication.

We have made clear that agreement on the banning of all nuclear-weapons tests, under effective verification and control, is a desirable end. I think that by taking such initiative toward disarmament, we are accurately expressing the American spirit of concern for humanity and peace. We are responding also to some very practical concerns. The world annually spends more than $120 billion on industries related to war and destruction — a figure greater than the total annual income of the poorer half of the world. This is a shocking waste of resources, even more so since none of the smaller countries can buy, with the military dollar, more than passing security against another small neighbor. And no one can buy security against large-scale aggression in this nuclear age.

The path toward disarmament is hard and tortuous. But as our quest gains ground, we will find innumerable other benefits, aside from relief that the threat of universal destruction has receded.

Civilian (peaceful) uses of nuclear energy need far more rapid development. Almost twenty years after the first atomic explosions, the peaceful applications of nuclear energy — so widely heralded — have not yet fulfilled their promise. I recall the newspaper and magazine articles of the late 1940's promising great miracles for mankind through the use of atomic energy. Some are, indeed, coming to pass. But a concentrated effort to develop peaceful uses of the atom has had comparatively low priority. With the elimination of some of our overriding defense needs, this peaceful application would rank high among the tasks assigned to our now defense-oriented industries.

The space race, for example, is essentially a military effort now. I think the military has a vital role in space — but I do not think it ought to own space. While space exploration is one of the legitimate tasks of the future, I wonder about the enormous amounts we are pouring into our present unilateral attempts. There are too many unmet needs on earth to have all those resources directed outside the atmosphere. Instead of trying to find out how dry it is on the moon, we would do well to try to find out, for example, how to put water into the soil. I have seen much American capital spent in undeveloped areas where the chief problem was lack of water. A concentrated, highly organized program on the study of water supply or on converting sea water into potable water could solve a major world problem.

There are countless such needs, right here on earth, to be met in our time. There are countless miracles in the peaceful use of nuclear energy to be wrought in our time.

We are certain of the superiority of our economic and political system. We welcome the competition to produce the goods and food sorely needed by much of the world, to find the markets, to reach the people. This healthy competition has been deferred and diverted by that ghastly contest: Who can make the most destructive nuclear weapons?

The realization that there are no winners in such a contest has made a measure of disarmament probable. And it has brought us closer to the peaceful competition we seek in order to demonstrate which system can really better man's lot.

Trade and the Cold War

In a sense, World War III — or at least a supremely important battle of the nuclear age — has already taken place. All the tensions and rivalry of the Cold War seemed about to erupt into nuclear explosion at the time of the Cuban missile crisis, in October, 1962. Then the great confrontation took place. The Soviet Union and the United States took full stock of each other's strength — military, economic, and psychological —

and of each other's determination to fight to the end. For a few days all the world awaited the outcome.

Our strength and determination prevailed. An agreement was reached to cover the specific situation — but its implications were world-wide. This nuclear-age armistice was different from all previous ones: It was agreed upon before, not after, the killing of millions of civilians and soldiers.

Since then, there have been a number of important steps in the easing of tensions. The limited test-ban treaty was concluded. Great Britain, the United States, and the Soviet Union agreed not to orbit nuclear weapons in outer space. The "hot line" was installed between the White House and the Kremlin to permit rapid communication in the event of emergency. And, finally, the United States agreed to sell up to $250 million worth of wheat to Russia, when its harvest failures made the importation of wheat necessary for Russia.

These steps were accompanied by the easing of the propaganda battle and a lessening of Soviet pressures generally. And since the missile crisis, neither the United States nor Russia appears to want another showdown involving the threat of nuclear war.

While none of these developments have brought us closer together on basic issues, they have improved the atmosphere of our relations with the Communist world. The basic issues seem to defy solution for the present: We have far to go before any real agreement is reached in the field of disarmament and on the status of Berlin and the division of Germany. And we have not seen any signs that the Soviets have abandoned their drive to spread Communist rule.

However, the atmosphere created by these recent developments is favorable for the exploration of further steps toward reducing tensions. We now have good reason to assume that the Soviet leadership is interested in backing away from its dangerous game. Important things are happening inside the Soviet Union and the satellite nations of Eastern Europe. Every perceptive visitor who has had the opportunity to compare current impressions with those of previous years comes back convinced that the curtain is lifting in Eastern Europe, however slowly or cautiously.

I have some firsthand acquaintance with the mind and plans of today's ruler of the Kremlin. In December, 1958, I met with Premier Khrushchev in Moscow for an eight-and-a-half-hour talk. Our informal meeting was fascinating, covering a huge range of subjects, including the American political scene. Mr. Khrushchev is a complicated human being, with many moods. He is also a consummate politician, with many motives. He is astonishingly well-informed about us. One of his sources is *The New York Times*, flown to the Kremlin daily and translated for him. I made a point of telling him that I had been fighting Communism for twenty years in one way or another; I wanted him to know that I was familiar with his philosophy and was against it. His attitude in response was "Good —

now we can talk, for we each know where we stand."

I once heard an American official describe Premier Khrushchev and the Russians as having "Oriental minds." There is a racist connotation in the term, and it is simply nonsense. There is no such thing as an "Oriental mind" in the sense used here; the Russians are human beings just as we are. We may find them hard to understand, because their culture and value systems are different from ours, but their emotional, spiritual, and physical needs are much the same as ours. They are our fellow human beings, and we must find ways to communicate fully with them.

Mr. Khrushchev is a practical politician as well as a dictator — a new combination for the Russians, and something new for us to deal with. He is also the kind of man who, if he had been born in this country, could have been a political boss or the head of a poltical machine, and would have been a very good political campaigner and debater. He cannot be equated with Hitler, who was utterly mad and depraved, or with Stalin, who was completely ruthless even with his own people and built a monstrous citadel of terror and oppression. Khrushchev is profoundly dedicated to the triumph of his system, but, as he showed at the time of the Cuban missile crisis, he is not irresponsible when it comes to the matter of the survival of mankind.

Khrushchev and Soviet leaders generally now seem to be more rational in their approach to world affairs. Perhaps they have been shocked by the cynicism of Communist China and that nation's apparent indifference to the possibilities of nuclear holocaust. As the split between the Soviet Union and China deepens — as I believe it must continue to do — we shall find more and more opportunity for communication and, perhaps, greater understanding of the government and people of the Soviet Union.

The Soviets are showing a measure of willingness for this to happen. The Voice of America is being allowed to get through freely to the Soviet people for the first time in many years. Soviet citizens in increasing numbers are permitted to travel outside the country. Western books and newspapers are allowed to circulate, although in highly restricted fashion. The secret police are no longer omnipresent. There is evidence that an intellectual ferment is under way.

Communist policy is changing because the traditional Communist tactics have not been effective. This is evident in the recent failures of Soviet agriculture, the rising demands of consumers, the restiveness of the intellectuals, and the emergence of the managerial elite — the "new class" described so vividly by the former Vice President of Yugoslavia, Milovan Djilas.

We need to keep in close contact with all elements of Soviet society. We need to increase suitable programs of cultural exchange. And we need, above all, to review our policy of trade with the Communist world, for such trade has vast significance and many ramifications.

The wheat sale was a beginning. Now, if we move

carefully in the direction of a more permissive trade policy with Eastern Europe, we shall be putting Soviet intentions in the field of international cooperation to a genuine test. We will know whether Russia is, indeed, prepared to abandon its past sterile policy of hostility and expansionism in favor of something more constructive.

Our trade policy in the past has been essentially punitive, designed to retaliate against and to discourage Soviet international "adventurism." Ever since the early postwar years, when Stalin set out deliberately to expand the perimeter of world Communism, we have used our commercial power in the effort to halt the growth of Communism. We knew then, on the basis of all our experience, that Soviet leaders were hopelessly committed to a course of forcible annexation of territory as the only way of demonstrating the inevitability of Communism. They were willing to sacrifice the elementary economic needs of their own people in this quest for territorial and political aggrandizement. These were hardly conditions calculated to make Russia any kind of commercial partner.

Today, the situation appears to be quite different. For one thing, Russia's leaders have apparently learned the hard lesson that a government cannot indefinitely substitute promises for basic needs if it is to endure and gain acceptance. They seem now to be standing at a critical juncture in their relations with their own people; the promises made over the decades have to be cashed in at last, or they run the risk of a general disenchantment, a severe decline in public morale, or worse.

The Soviet Union is also faced with the massive failures of its agricultural system; in spite of its conscious pursuit of economic self-sufficiency for decades, it has failed completely to achieve self-sufficiency in feeding its own people.

Until the American wheat sale to the Soviet Union, our trade policy remained based on the most rigid possible concept. It took no account of the changes from Stalin to Khrushchev, of the implications of the Sino-Soviet split, of the lessening of American-Russian tensions.

The nations of Western Europe, since the end of the Korean War, have not shared our highly restrictive standards for the control of exports to Eastern Europe. We did share an effective common policy with them, withholding strategic goods from the Soviet bloc, from 1949 to 1954, years of maximum peril to the West. But our free-world friends have long since changed their policy. All exports from the free world to Russia in 1950 amounted to $300 million. In 1962, they amounted to $1.8 billion.

Western Europe has chosen to withhold only a limited list of strategic goods, while our export control has extended over a wide range of industrial equipment and materials.

The situation is anomalous. Many of the same types of goods denied export licenses by us have been legally sold and shipped to the Soviet Union and its satellites by manufacturers in Western

Europe. The disparity in export policy between the United States and Western Europe has, in most cases, nullified our attempts to withhold goods from the Soviet-block countries. With some notable exceptions, most types of industrial equipment needed by them have been available in Western Europe.

A few 1962 statistics will illustrate the gap that has developed between the level of our exports to the Soviet bloc and those of Western Europe:

The total value of goods we exported to Eastern Europe was $125 million; Western Europe exported goods valued at $2.1 billion — about 16 times more.

In the key category of machinery and transport equipment, our exports to Eastern Europe amounted to $7.6 million; exports from Western Europe amounted to $756.3 million — a ratio of 100 to 1.

There is a still sharper disparity in the case of manufactured goods: $21 million worth from the United States and $675.5 million from Western Europe — 300 to 1.

Obviously, a tremendous amount of American business is being lost through such a restrictive trade policy — and to no advantage at all, since the needs of the European Communist countries are largely being met despite our efforts to the contrary. The U.S. Chamber of Commerce recognized this fact when, in April, 1964, it urged our government to cut back the list of items barred from sale to the Soviet Union and the other East European nations.

In their trade with Communist countries, the West European nations abide by a list agreed to by an Allied Coordinating Committee; it is limited to items of clear military significance. It was a major policy innovation for the U.S. Chamber of Commerce to call upon the government to change its policy on the grounds that the effect of our longer embargo list "has not been to deprive the Communist countries of goods but to divert business to European suppliers."

The Chamber called for a level of American trade equal to that of our European allies. If adopted by the government, the Chamber's proposal would mean freeing hundreds of items — ranging from oil refineries to most types of machinery — for sale to the Soviet Union and its East European satellites. (There would be no change in the outright embargo on exports to Communist China, North Korea, North Vietnam, and Cuba, although some Chamber delegates did support a proposal for trade with all Communist nations.)

The Chamber rejected an amendment that would have required payment in gold for all exports to Communist countries; as it stands now, its resolution permits "ordinary commercial credit."

This is a basic point, since the trade of the free world, particularly that of the industrialized countries of Western Europe and Japan, depends upon the extension of credits. If we are to participate in this expanding trade, American business, in order to compete, will have to provide credit financing. Free-world firms have been extending credit to Communist-bloc countries for periods ranging from one to ten years. In the last five years, this credit has amounted to an amerage of about $350 million annually. At least three-quarters of the credit by private firms was guaranteed — insured by governmental or quasi-governmental organizations in the exporting country.

The present level of United States trade with the Communist bloc is insignificant, representing less than seven-tenths of 1 per cent of our total exports. Under present trade policies, we are barred from competing for a share of the more than $4-billion-a-year market represented by the bloc. Between 80 and 90 per cent of the commodities making up that figure could be licensed for export from the United States. Soviet-bloc countries have indicated an interest in a variety of American commodities and technical data. Often, even when an export license is obtainable for them, our firms still cannot compete with those of Western Europe because of their inability to operate in the credit market — even when the goods are competitive in price. Without credit, of course, only a minimum of cash purchases will be made by bloc countries in the United States.

We have a serious balance-of-payments problem, although it appears to be improving. We must make every effort to help American businessmen and farmers compete with those of Western Europe and Japan. The fact that these nations have extended credits to the Soviet bloc and that their trade has grown in the space of five years from $2.6 billion to $4.1 billion suggests that the bloc countries are good commercial risks. United States trade in peaceful goods with this area could amount to several hundred million dollars annually, and possibly much more.

Increased trade would have the important by-product of increased contact — and contact could eventually lead to greater understanding. This is the premise for our program of cultural exchange; it is equally valid for extension of trade to the East European nations.

We must live in this world and seek to improve it in any way we can. I know that some persons believe that the best way to deal with Communism is simply to hate it or ignore it, hoping that it will go away. But real life is simply not that way.

We have gotten over the idea that all Russians are ignorant peasants who don't know how to repair the machinery the Western world has given them. (The first Sputnik demolished that myth.) And we have gotten over the converse idea that Russians are indomitable supermen — an idea that reflected a singular lack of faith in ourselves and our system.

I am in favor of competition in all possible ways with the Communist world. But I believe, too, in trade and exchange of all kinds when trade and exchange serve our self-interest. Self-interest happens to include peace as well as profit.

Beyond that, I believe that any policy, foreign or domestic, based solely on anti-Communism is an edifice built on sand. Today, the world does not so much need massive weapons systems as it needs massive programs of understanding, of health, food, and education. And it needs the superlative products of the American economic system.

VII

Liberalism and National Security

The search for world peace, particularly the search for a world order in which nuclear weapons would not threaten the obliteration of our civilization, has been a task of overriding importance and constant concern in the dangerous years since Hiroshima. But there is nothing contradictory about striving for peace and at the same time being determined to defend our nation and our national interests. Indeed, while some liberals are pacifists, liberalism is not pacifism. Most American liberals stand in the ranks of those who believe that the forces of totalitarianism must be met with the forces of free men. In a world of imperfect men and imperfect nations, individuals and nations must be prepared to defend themselves. Liberalism recognizes the fundamental obligation of government to maintain order and to provide for the common defense.

Liberal groups in America for the past

twenty-five years have conspicuously and consistently supported the building up, the maintenance, and the use, when necessary, of enormous military forces in the face of the threats from fascism and Communism. But liberals have also stressed that the nation's security does not depend solely upon the size of the armed services, the number of thermonuclear delivery systems, or the dollar amount of the Department of Defense budget. There is no security in a great arms race — only an increasingly volatile insecurity in which one side's mistake may escalate into mutual destruction. Therefore, while determined not to fall behind in the arms race, we have also sought every reasonable means possible to slow it down and to bring it to a halt without weakening our security. Safeguarded arms control and disarmament have been viewed as the reverse side of the coin of national security. The objective of both the military planner and the arms-control planner is the safety and security of our people.

The concept of total disarmament is founded on a vision of the world and a view of man's development as they may be in some distant future. Just as no serious person would argue that any city government in America could maintain order without an efficient police force, it cannot be argued successfully that all the differences between nation-states can be settled at the conference table in a sanitized environment, free from any hint of the use of armed force. Rather, the present objective should be to return to a sane and reasonable level of military forces, including provisions for mutual inspection to guard against an arms buildup or a sudden attack.

But world peace cannot be ensured simply by the reduction of the arms of the superpower. In a world that is increasingly multipolar, the threat of violence and disorder in many areas demands a buildup of international police forces — international fire brigades, if you will — to bring explosive situations under control, to restore order, and to deter terrorism. Whatever may be its form, operating under whatever sovereignty, there will remain for the foreseeable future the need for military ground, air, naval, and marine forces that can defend the right of self-determination of nations, that can come to the rescue of legal governments threatened by over-the-border aggression or externally guided insurgency, or that can step between two unreasoning antagonists in the interest of peace. The United Nations, at the moment, appears to offer the best possibility for the establishment of a multination police force on a permanent basis.

Clearly, the outward thrust of Communism has demanded and will continue to demand very heavy investments in national defense. But it is important to stress that times change, antagonists change, old enemies can become friends, and friends can become estranged; therefore, the armed forces of the United States must not be organized and maintained on the basis of worn-out conceptions and doctrines. The wrong arms policy can actually reduce, rather than increase, the national security. And the very weight and power of a giant military establishment and its supporting industrial complex can become a determinant of the national foreign policy, rather than a servant of that policy.

That is why I so strongly advocate the principle of civilian supremacy in the armed services — and the supremacy of foreign policy over military policy. A gigantic officer corps can, without any thought of conspiracy, become the *de facto* desicion-makers of the nation's foreign policy — unless there are alert and strong-minded men in the Department of State, the Department of Defense, and, above all, the office of the President. Indeed, because of the huge amounts of Federal money they disburse to industry, the officer corps of the armed services already exert a powerful influence on the industrial economy and, willy-nilly, on the political life of the nation. Many officers in the services share a concern for the principle of civilian supremacy. Indeed, it is a remarkable tribute to the selection process of the officer corps that so many of the highest-ranking officers of the various services have been among the most vigorous and brilliant exponents of the principle that the military must *serve* the nation, rather than dominate it.

At the same time, the exercise of civilian control over the services must be such as to encourage the initiative and the *elan* of the officer corps. We ask a great deal of the officers and men of our armed forces, and we pay them little enough in the way of income and recognition. Ultimately, it will be they who make the battlefield decisions in any war or police action in which we may find ourselves. A civilian policy that crosses the line from firm policy direction into the area of interference in the normal military chain of command can have only one effect: the discouragement of initiative and daring and the loss to civilian pursuits of some of the finest minds and characters among the officer corps. In the final anlysis, we must depend on the officer corps to come up with professional proposals, to try out the weapons developed by the government or industry (or both) on the firing ranges and perhaps in actual combat, and to command the ground, sea, and air forces.

The principle of competition advocated in the realm of economics and other nonmilitary areas should be followed in the management and guidance of the Defense Department as well. Far too much has been heard about "wrangling" and "cutthroat competition" among the services. The fact is that the defense of the nation is an extraordinarily complex and costly undertaking; and the consequences of an error of omission or commission are so great that the competition of ideas among the services should be vigorously stimulated rather than discouraged. Granted, decisions must be made, and timely decisions. But those decisions should be made, not by a chief of staff of all the armed services, but by the President as Commander in Chief and by his civilian assistants and advisers, after they have been exposed to the perhaps conflicting viewpoints of the Joint Chiefs of Staff. Indeed, the proposal for a single chief of staff is a serious threat to the principle of civilian supremacy over the armed services, for it would deny to the President the benefit of vigorous discussion and debate among the services on matters of supreme national importance.

The bureaucracies of the services and of the Department of Defense itself already tend to stifle very fresh and constructive ideas before they work themselves to the top; to compound the problem by forcing all army, air, and naval thinking into one final conduit would seriously impair the intellectual vitality of the entire officer corps. Certainly, it could tend to promote rigid, doctrinaire thinking and to the creation of armed forces unable to adapt rapidly to changing conditions. And in a world in which international relationships are increasingly transitory and subject to surprising changes, the qualities called for are imagination and initiative, speed and flexibility.

While the overriding threat to our nation, to all of civilization, is the presence in the world of large numbers of deliverable nuclear and thermonuclear weapons, it is clear that no sane ruler will deliberately risk the certain obliteration of his own country by initiating an attack with such weapons. Increasingly, then, the odds favor conflict in which nuclear weapons play no role other than to prevent the delibreate use of such weapons by an antagonist. Conflict with a Communist power then becomes ever more complex and sophisticated, with a wide spectrum of confrontation, ranging from economic sanctions, to terrorism and insurgency, to traditional political action, to the possibility of large-scale non-nuclear warfare. The forces of the armed services must be considered as only part of the arsenal of the President, to be utilized along with a whole complex of political and economic forces of his command. Needless to say, the more flexible and resilient, the more imaginative and creative the armed services are, the more valuable they will be to a President's foreign policy.

Force is present in the world. The only tenable position of a liberal is that despite reluctance to use it unless all other courses are exhausted, one must still be prepared and willing to use force.

When President Betancourt of Venezuela, a distinguished liberal, was faced with open terrorism, he used his armed forces to defend his government and to preserve free elections — setting a stirring example for the world.

Free government cannot stand unless it is prepared to defeat aggression from without or within. Liberalism becomes a mockery when it is spineless and cowardly. No slogans, no long-range policies offering economic and social progress can defeat the threat of immediate, naked force — in the streets, from the air, from the sea. Only force itself — and the willingness to use it swiftly, powerfully, and courageously — can maintain a free government in power when subversion and terrorism are used against it.

Even more important, though, is the fact that military force *alone* is relatively helpless against a determined and intelligent exploitation of a people's despair and hopelessness. The shield of military defense — while it may stave off disaster for a time — must be used to support a program of genuine progress and reform, or totalitarianism may eventually take hold of a nation. A people who will not fight for its government of its own free will cannot be pressed successfully into combat against insurgent forces. The whole concept of U.S. military aid to prevent a nation from "going Communist" founders when not accompanied by at least an equal effort in the political, economic, and social areas. We must count on the American officers who serve as advisers in counter-insurgency efforts in foreign lands to tell us what the needs and aspirations of the people are so that we can devise programs and policies that will aid those people and give them the will to fight. This is the case in Vietnam, and no doubt there will be other parts of the world where once again the strategies and tactics of Communist penetration will be tested against the abilities of free men to defeat them.

We should have learned from our internal struggles against Communist penetration (and we had a sharp and severe political battle with the Communist Party during my own early years in Minnesota politcs) that Communist determination is strong. We should have learned from our efforts to stem Communist subversion in Latin America, the Middle East, Africa, and Southeast Asia that the enemy is ingenious and calculating, and that he will utilize every political, economic, and military weapon at his command.

We should have learned that the Communist

ideology cannot be beaten by defending a decadent and immoral society, and that the finest weapons cannot prevail when they are in the hands of those who do not want to defend themselves.

We are learning, slowly and painfully, through the experience of tens of thousands of men and women who are working in the villages, in the city slums, and in the jungle wildernesses — some bearing arms and some bringing medicine, education, food, and instruction in political and economic organization. To these Americans, some in the armed services and some civilians, we owe gratitude beyond measure. For under the umbrella of nuclear deterrence, they are carrying on the ultimate struggle in the "third world" for the security of the United States.

VIII

The Government and the People

With all our concern for the world about us, Americans seem to have started looking within more deeply in the past few months. The war against poverty, the issue of civil rights, the problems of education and of utilizing our domestic resources have occupied more of our time.

The lessening of Cold War tensions has

something to do with this. The effects are constructive and good. We need greater reforming zeal and accomplishment at home if we are to be effective in our relationships with the rest of the world. In the past, we have made preachments and demands abroad while our own house was in disorder. We have been in the indefensible position of telling other governments how to act while we suffered McCarthyism at home, of expressing concern for the morality of people abroad while we had our Little Rocks at home.

We are now doing our housecleaning. We are looking within — not to disentangle ourselves from commitments abroad, but eventually to show a better American face to the world. The war on poverty and the fight for human rights are prime examples of what we are doing at home. And increasingly, even the things we do abroad are proof of a growing sense of national purpose and domestic morality. Our Peace Corps, unprecendented among nations, is an example of how we are reaffirming our idealism, getting away from platitudes, digging in with spirit and heart.

It is urgent that we do this. We must appear to be — and actually be — more concerned with issues of moral principle. An apparent lack of integrity has shown often enough. Our friends abroad have occasionally looked upon us in horror, not just for domestic blemishes, but for our acts and associations in various parts of the world.

For example, we have a policy on Cuba: We want to eliminate Castroism. But many people are skeptical about what we want *after* Castro. It is important that throughout Cuba and all Latin America it be fully understood that we want Castro's Communist regime to be replaced with a progressive government. A Cuban government dedicated to political liberty and economic and social reforms will have the firm support of the United States. Another tyrannical government of the extreme right will not.

We must make this clear because we have, in the past, sometimes allied ourselves with corrupt regimes whose leadership was just one step ahead of a firing squad. We have committed sins of political expediency. Because of this, there has been some cynicism about our motives and a feeling in many areas that we were no longer to be identified with people's aspirations for freedom.

It is good that we have again begun to look within. One area that needs this introspective view is the relationship between the government and the American people. It is a vital area, and what we do to improve it — and to improve the functioning of our government itself — is basic to a flourishing democracy.

The Need for Planning

This is in many ways a different world and a different America from those of my boyhood. Government, particularly, lives in a new and ever-changing environment. One may well look at our democratic institutions today and ask: "Has our legislative machinery and the legislative process adjusted itself to its new responsibilities?"

The relationship between the Federal and state governments is a great and important problem, but the relationships inside the Federal Government — among the judicial, legislative, and executive branches — pose a problem that requires even more careful analysis. Far too little attention is given to the role of Congressional responsibility. The many criticisms that have been leveled at recent sessions of Congress demonstrate what is happening to Congressional responsibility, Congressional power, and Congressional adequacy.

We must look beyond mere mechanical refinements of the legislative process or of the executive operation. We need to understand more clearly the relationship of people in a representative democracy to their government. There is dead air space, a gulf, between the people and the government, causing serious political and social consequences. Respect for law and order, faith in representative government, confidence in national policy are engendered by tested and accepted institutions and allegiance to the Constitution. But they are also fostered by the conviction that government can translate into action the popular will or the national consensus. The gap that has developed between the people and their government is by far a great threat to our system and our social structure than any external threat.

One manifestation of the gap, of course, is the civil-rights issue. Millions of people who have the obligations of citizenship have not been given the privileges of citizenship; millions of people have felt excluded from the protection of the law when they were not able to participate fully in the decision-making process of popular sovereignty.

The gap has been expanded by those who have preached the doctrine that the Federal Government is the enemy of the people. This doctrine has bordered on outright hatred, prejudice, and bigotry in some cases, as evidenced by the statements of the extreme right. Politics has been described so often as a dirty business that we tend to forget that representative government is not expected to produce an elite, or a group of philospher-kings, or a congress of saints and angels. Representative government represents the good and the bad, the clean and the dirty, the excellent, the mediocre, and the poor. Our duty is to set high standards and to insist upon excellence, even from those who never demonstrated it before their election to responsibility.

One of the most hopeful things that has happened to our representative government in recent years was the far-reaching Supreme Court decision on Congressional reapportionment, assuring more adequate, honorable, and just representation to the voters of the states. It is particularly important because the population explosion in the United States is radically altering the character of the electorate. By 1980, there will be more than 260 million of us. We are coalescing and clustering in giant urban complexes. By 1980, there will be more than 80 million persons living in only one of these great urban chains — stretching along the Eastern Seaboard from Boston to

Washington, D.C. Another such chain will run along the rim of the Great Lakes from Buffalo to Chicago. The population cluster in Florida and some other spots along the Gulf Coast will intensify and thicken. A few inladn webs will develop around the Twin Cities of Minnesota, around Denver, Salt Lake City, and Phoenix. And there will be a massive movement of population to the West.

By 1980, the face of the Congress will be greatly altered by these changes in population. Cities will be underrepresented in the Senate, but they will dominate the House membership. The recent projections for 1980 prepared by the U.S. Bureau of the Census show these major changes in the House of Representatives: a shift of power to the great city areas all across the board; a shift of power clearly westward beyond the mountain states and to the West Coast; the Midwest barely holding its own; the states of the South, the border states, New England, and the large Middle Atlantic states losing representation.

A few examples: The South will lose 10 per cent or more of its House seats. The border states will lose almost 15 per cent of their House seats. New England will lose more than 15 per cent of its House seats. Texas and Florida, with their fast-growing cities, will pick up about 15 per cent more than their present House seats. The mountain states will pick up another 15 per cent in their representation. The West Coast, with the addition of more than ten seats, will register a gain of almost 20 per cent in the House. Virtually every new seat in Congress will be one representing a large city.

In short, by the time the toddlers of today are able to vote, the House of Representatives will be a body measurably more Western and much more urban-oriented. A major proportion of the population will have no contact with or understanding of rural America, although the literature and the culture of our democracy have always been oriented around the small rural town or the middle-sized community.

What will this mean to Congress in such matters as planning? What will happen in city planning — not just conventional city planning, but vast regional and area planning? To cite one small hazard: It is almost impossible today to get the Congress of the United States to say anything about open spaces in its legislation for urban renewal or urban housing. Are we to condemn people to live on strips of concrete for lack of proper planning?

So long as public planning is shunned as being vaguely un-American, we are committing ourselves to a mangled, expensive, and uncertain future. In the fields of transportation, for example, simply building ribbons of highways will not ultimately solve our traffic problems. Despite the population projections facing us, we are not now able to plan the engineering studies that will help move people from their homes to their jobs. The massive waste of time, money, and energy caused by faulty transportation makes the Federal deficit fade into insignificance.

What about our agricultural patterns? We can produce all the food and fiber that this nation needs in the foreseeable future with one-half of the people now on the farms. Our farms today are sending a steady outpouring of their population to the cities. American agricultural efficiency has staffed our factories and populated our cities.

What about the dispersal of industry? What happens in mid-America? What about financing and credit for those vast areas of America from which population seems to be drifting away? They will have little or no representation in the House of Representatives. Who will speak for them?

We may be faced with a backwash of areas of chronic unemployment; people cannot always pick up and leave just because a blueprint says they should. Many things hold people to communities when there is no economic base — family, age, sentiment, or just an inability to liquidate and get out. Increased efficiency of workers, wholesale changes in raw-material production, the technological revolution in agricultural methods are releasing millions of people to our cities and frequently to unemployment.

City people do not need to be reminded that their air is getting foul, their water is a problem both in purity and in sufficiency, their surroundings are either unplanned or inadequately planned (and are sometimes ugly and depressing), their educational systems are having difficulties, their transportation and communication lag behind population needs. I do not need to remind them that the central cities and the suburbs are dividing along lines of race and class, and that this built-in erosion of democracy is intolerable. We can see it happening with the massive migration of

Negroes into the core cities of the North and West from the rural slums of the South. To deal with all these urban problems, we have almost hopeless mazes of city governments, suburban councils, county governments, and state authorities, which try to stay afloat with stop-gap measures, inadequate tax bases, uncertain jurisdictions, and less than friendly and understanding legislators.

Yet these tough domestic problems are less important than the problem of achieving world peace. The military power of the United States has been a shield for the protection of that peace, but armed power alone is a bleak and uncertain insurance against the holocaust of thermonuclear war. Many of us fail to recognize the impact of twenty-five years of military mobilization upon democratic institutions. It was difficult enough for this republic to face a depression in the 1930's, even under the dynamic leadership of a Franklin Roosevelt. The experience of those years tested democratic institutions, but it also invigorated and strengthened them. I find very few examples in history, though, where prolonged military mobilization — and the fear, suspicion, doubt, and uncertainty that are part of and often the cause of military mobilization — have strengthened democratic institutions. We should be searching within our own experience to learn how we can maintain the military strength necessary in an uncertain world, and at the same time strengthen the democratic institutions that this mobilization is designed to protect and defend. I am not sure that we have found the answers — including an answer to the problem of the military-industrial complex, which President Dwight Eisenhower raised in his farewell address.

Some day we may face the possibility of the Soviet Union's taking a bolder leap toward disarmament than any now hoped for. If it were to propose genuine disarmament with the safeguards that we consider essential, we would all be ill-prepared to seize the opportunity. Unless some steps are taken along the lines I have suggested for a major Commission on Automation, Technology, and Employment, we are going to suffer an almost total absence of planning to offset the impact of a possible major arms reduction on our economy. What would happen if there were to be in the next two years a $25 billion cut in Federal defense expenditures? What happens to whole cities when there is as much as a $100 million reduction in Federal spending for space programs?

Surely our country cannot be put in the position of rejecting the path to peace through safeguarded disarmament simply because we cannot afford the economic adjustments that a slowdown or shutdown in defense expenditures would require. Planning for the conversion from defense industry to peacetime industry is an absolute essential. Yet our government is still unprepared, and so are most of our communities.

Nor are we properly equipped to cope with the revolutionary ferment stirring in the societies of Latin America, Africa, and Asia. There are new needs and new demands, new power structures with which we are still unfamiliar. "Those who make peaceful revolution impossible," President Kennedy said, "make a violent one inevitable."

The United States of America, born in revolution, dedicated to progressive thought, committed to liberal democratic institutions throughout its entire history, should be the nation most capable today of understanding the methodology of a peaceful revolution or of how it is to be accomplished.

Because we have failed to plan and contemplate the future, we have left the doctrine of revolution to the reactionaires and to the brutes and the tyrants. The revolution of democracy has become a chapter in our history, not often enough a page of living faith and living practice. All the foreign aid we can give will not help us — or the recipients either — until we know the kind of world in which we want to live, the kind of philosophy that should motivate men's actions. We have been long on money, but short on thought. We have dreamed the great and beautiful dream of a better world. But we have avoided real planning for it; so long as we do, it will continue to elude us.

The Needs of Congress

Can democratic representative government really meet the problems outlined in the preceding pages? I think so. But fundamental improvements are going to have to be made. The Federal Government cannot do the entire job alone, nor should it, but it does have a special and real responsibility that most of our people must recognize.

The task of the Congress is to deal with such critical matters, domestic and foreign, and at the same time to maintain rapport with the people. Congress must therefore know more, and the people must be more fully informed. Congress needs to streamline its procedures. Newton Minow told me that, as Chairman of the Federal Communications Commission, he had to testify on the communications-satellite bill before thirteen separate committees and subcommittees of the Congress. How can the people expect effective administration if agency heads are engaged in a long-distance race, speeding back and forth among committees, attempting to educate and inform — or just to communicate — with a handful here, a handful there?

Congressional committees and subcommittees should not be as jealous of their jurisdiction as they are concerned with solutions. (I speak as a practitioner of the legislative process.) One improvement in this area would be the formation of more joint committees at the subcommittee level, thus conserving the time of our administrators. But the greatest problem in the Congress today is how to equip ourselves more effectively to handle matters of national security, matters of peace and war.

I have three proposals to help meet the problem. One is for a Joint Committee on National Security. After World War II, President Truman established the National Security Council within the executive branch. He did so because he had to bring together the Secretary of State with the Secretary of Defense, the Chairman of the Council of Economic Advisers with the Secretary of the Treasury. In other words, he had to bring into the decision-making process of the executive branch of the government the conflicting ideas of the separate jurisdictions so that they could be harmonized.

But what do we have in Congress? The nuclear-test-ban treaty provides a good example. The decision to sign the treaty was made in the National Security Council after conflicting ideas were worked out, after information was exchanged within the confines of this established Council mechanism, after the opinions and attitudes of the Joint Chiefs of Staff were explored. Without this kind of coordination of thinking and of policy through one organized body, there would have been a thousand voices and a thousand different proposals.

Then the treaty came to the Senate. Had it followed regular procedures, it would have passed through at least the following jurisdictions: the Armed Services Committee, the Armed Services Special Subcommittee on Preparedness, the Joint Committee on Atomic Energy, the Foreign Relations Committee. It was only because of an *ad hoc* arrangement suggested by Senator Fulbright (that the committees be pooled into one for the hearings) that we were able to finish the discussions in six weeks.

If Congress is to have anything substantially more than a negative voice on foreign policy, it needs a Joint Committee on National Security as a counterpart of the executive branch's National Security Council. It would be composed of those who now have the main responsibility in the committees relating to trade, disarmament, armament, diplomacy — members of the Atomic Energy Committee, the Appropriations

Committee, the Foreign Relations Committee, and the Military Affairs or Armed Services Committee. Today, when members of Congress are doubtful about some executive action, their automatic relfex is to say No. The way to remove doubt is through information.

Another improvement the Congress can make is the establishment of a permanent Joint Committee on Congressional Organization and Operations for constant review, on a year-by-year basis, of the institutions of the Congress. The effort would be to upgrade them. I can offer some personal insight into the need for improvement:

I consider my life to be at least up to the average standard in Congressional activity. I receive more than a thousand letters every day in the week. I have hundreds of visitors, because the jet plane has brought a Senator's whole constituency within a few hours of his office. I receive no fewer than seventy long-distance calls from constituents every day of my life, not to mention the calls from my colleagues. How does one find time to tend to pressing duties of Congress?

Absenteeism in committees and on the floor of Congress does not arise from the laziness of the members; it occurs because they are some other place at the insistence of their constituents. I have to fight for time even to get to those committees of which I am chairman. Why are the members of the Senate not in the Senate? They are not out on the golf course. They are in subcommittee or committee, or, just as likely, back in their offices with a backlog of visitors and mail and telephone calls.

The members of Congress have become the brokers between the executive branch and the people. The executive branch — what most people consider the "government" — is big and maze-like, and people do not know where to go. They have lost contact, except through their Congressman or Senator. We spend our time trying to get a Social Security check for a person who should already have had it, or getting a veteran into a hospital when he ought to have been admitted in the first place. There are thousands of such cases each year. Congress is so overworked that the whole process gets bottlenecked, and all we can do is to try somehow to meet the most immediate problems that beset us.

If I work less than fourteen hours a day, I feel that I have denied both my work and my official duty. It is utterly impossible to work less. To be effective, it is helpful if you are intelligent, but it is more helpful if you are *there* where the decisions are made, in the subcommittees or the committees. But, of course, we will not even have a chance to be at the subcommittees if we are not seeing the people who sent us to Congress in the first place.

My third proposal revolves around finding some way of bringing to the Congress the brain power, the reservoir of intellect and expertise, that modern government requires. We have a government of separation of powers, of checks and balances. There are certainly plenty of checks; Congress can balk and stop the government dead in its tracks. But what about balance? The balance between the legislative and executive branches can never be righted until the legislature has within its mechanism the kind of talent that the executive departments have long been able to attract.

The time is at hand to consider creating a new arm of Congress — a Congressional Institute consisting of a group of scholars who would serve the Congress as a pool of knowledge and thought.

Back in 1922, Walter Lippmann said that one of the difficulties with the Congress was that its members could not hope to master all they needed to know. There is today far more of a deplorable gap between what one needs to know and what one does know. The situation has become dangerous, and Congress is not equipped to handle it.

I have tried to learn everything I could about disarmament and its problems. But the Congress of the United States is barely qualified to assist any serious quest for knowledge on this vital subject; it has exactly one staff member working on disarmament! Fortunately, the executive branch has established an Arms Control and Disarmament Agency. Unfortunately, many members of Congress are suspicious of it. They need not be, but when a man is without information he acts from distrust or fear — and says No to the most legitimate request.

The Congress deals with a budget that will amount to almost $100 billion next year. How is it equipped to handle it? The Bureau of the Budget prepares and presents that budget. But the Congress has to decide on it. The Budget Bureau has thousands of employees. There are fewer than a hundred on the staffs of the Appropriations Committees of both houses of Congress. The best minds in the country should be examining this budget — and projecting ahead through the years: What does the population change mean in terms of the budget? Should the budget be the kind that we now have (about as antiquated as a smoke signal), or should we be looking forward to a kind of capital budget, as well as an expenditure budget?

This kind of thinking and planning must be tied into the Congressional process itself and become part of the establishment of government.

The proposed Congressional Institute should be staffed far beyond the size of the present Appropriations Committees. Perhaps a one-year to three-year term of service would permit scholars to rotate from the best institutions of higher learning. Such rotation would serve to maintain the vitality of ideas in Congress and in the university community as well.

Think of some of the issues that Congress must know more about, of the terms that must be defined before we can sensibly approach our tasks. Congress recently passed the tax bill. It should have been discussing long-range tax adjustments and tax policy years ago. We have no answers to the relationship between Federal and state revenues. We have not come to grips with the balance-of-payments problem, and everybody knows it. We scarcely know what we are talking about when we use the phrase "international liquidity." We have not the slightest idea of the capital needs of the world in which we live, much less how we are going to answer them. The private enterprise system of the United States will rise or fall on what we do internationally in terms of the fulfillment of capital needs and long-term credits for the growing population of the world. I should think that any number of bankers or merchants or manufacturers who love capitalism would say to their friends in Congress, "Good God, let's look ahead."

The scholars for such a Congressional Institute could be selected by their peers, the professional associations. Freedom of inquiry should be assured, so that there would be no directed verdicts. At the same time, Congress would retain the powers of decision, and individual committee staffs would have the responsibility for specific legislation. The executive branch has developed the use of scholars and has thus been able to provide some over-all designs and to make some long-range proposals. If the system of checks and balances is to have greater meaning, Congress must have the same kind of professional, scholarly support.

These are some of the ways we can help the legislative system to adapt to changing times. I have confidence in its toughness and flexibility to do so. Our experiment in representative government is being made on faith. In the end, I believe that it will prove to be the most efficient, responsive, and humane of all the political systems ever designed by man.

IX

A Personal Reflection

I am a man who enjoys life. There are far, far more things that I should like to do, to experience, to accomplish, than I shall ever have time for. Public service — to which I am devoted — denies a man as much, certainly, as it gives to him. The demands of this life are insatiable: There are never enough hours in the day, days in the week. Children grow up before one realizes how time has flown by. Often one feels frustrated by the sheer impossibility of leading a normal family life.

And in the political struggle, in the competition of ideas, in the swirl of controversy and the responsibility of decision-making, there do come to all men moments of hesitation, of a failing of self-confidence, of disillusionment and even exhaustion.

But in the highly charged world of American politics, there are also great joys and a magnificent sense of work being done, of problems being solved, of accomplishment. If it is hard work, it is good work. It is enterprise in the freest sense, where a man is continually risking his reputation and his record, where his judgment is constantly being tested, where his survival and success depend not only upon his ability but also upon his courage.

For more than twenty years of such public life, I

have tried to serve as a voice and a worker for the cause of equal justice and equal opportunity, for the general welfare, and for the common defense of our country. In all those years I have never felt truly alone. I have always been aware of the innate good sense and good will of the American people, and this awareness has buoyed me when prospects looked bleakest.

I am optimistic by nature, but I am also an optimist because if one can take the long view, one is stirred by the sense of progress, of improvement, of enlargement and enlightenment in this republic of ours. It is astonishing, for example, that the American people have been able throughout our nearly two centuries as a nation to call to leadership so many men of genuine nobility of purpose and strength of character, so many men of selfless dedication to the public good, so many men who have governed with wisdom and vision.

I have never doubted America and its people. And I have faith in the future of mankind. There is a common yearning for peace, for human dignity, for individual fulfillment that breaches the artificial barriers of nations, creeds, and political philosophies.

We have been passing through the darkest and most ominous period in recorded history, under the monstrous shadow of the mushroom-shaped cloud. Mankind has never before been threatened with such destructive power — the power not only to kill incalculable numbers of human beings, but also to distort and to pervert such life as might be left on the planet.

But I sense a growing consensus among the

leaders of the world community, a growing determination to turn away from the madness of a nuclear arms race into the paths of peace. In the past decade, particularly, there has been notable leadership given to this new and affirmative course of human history.

In the first years of the 1960's, four outstanding personalities who could truly be called world leaders because of the immense influence they had on the minds of men passed from this world in the midst of their efforts to advance a more humane, a more just, and a more rational relationship among nations. It is fitting that we should pause to pay tribute to them. Although two of them represent what is finest in the American character, the other two remind us that America has no monopoly on virtue and wisdom, and that the American nation is only a thread in the great tapestry of civilized humanity.

If we have made some progress out of that valley of the shadow of death in these past few years, surely these four men and women can claim much of our gratitude for that progress:

Dag Hammarskjold, who gave his life for the United Nations, working to prevent a civil war in the Congo — a man who was a symbol of rational world order, of the obligation of the advanced nations to help the newly independent nations find their way into paths of peace and freedom.

Eleanor Roosevelt, whose person and spirit were the very embodiment of the noble aspirations of all humanity, whose voice was the voice of man's innate compassion for those in need everywhere.

John XXIII, who in his brief reign as Supreme Pontiff of the Roman Catholic Church promulgated two of history's great documents on peace, *Pacem in Terris* and *Mater et Magistra*, calling on mankind's leaders to remember that we are all children of God.

John Fitzgerald Kennedy, thirty-fifth President of the United States, who was struck down as he was setting his nation firmly on the course toward security and peace. President Kennedy's great speech delivered at American University in the summer of 1963 was the ultimate expression of his purposeful and courageous foreign policy.

They are all gone. But who would say that these four lived in vain?

And who can doubt the future of the mankind that nourished them?